How To Live A Happily Ever Afterlife

Stories of Trapped Souls and How Not to Become One

ECHO BODINE

Foreword by Chip Coffey

HAMPTON ROADS

Cover design by Kathryn Sky-Peck
Cover art by iStock
Interior by Timm Bryson, em em design, LLC
Typeset in Adobe Jenson Pro

Hampton Roads Publishing Company, Inc.
Charlottesville, VA 22906
Distributed by Red Wheel/Weiser, LLC
www.redwheelweiser.com

Sign up for our newsletter and special offers by going to
www.redwheelweiser.com/newsletter.

ISBN: 978-1-64297-038-8
Library of Congress Cataloging-in-Publication Data available upon
request.

Printed in the United States of America
IBI
10 9 8 7 6 5 4 3 2 1

ALSO BY ECHO BODINE

Dear Echo

Echoes of the Soul

The Gift

Hands That Heal

The Key

The Little Book of True Ghost Stories

Look for the Good and You'll Find God

My Big Book of Healing

A Still, Small Voice

Things I Wish I'd Known When I Got Started

What Happens When We Die

TABLE OF CONTENTS

ACKNOWLEDGMENTS

First and foremost, I have to thank my brother, Michael Bodine, for helping me remember some of these stories. It was fun going back in time to some of the ghost adventures we've shared. Thank goodness for his nine-years-younger memory. It's getting a bit foggy in this old brain of mine.

Second, I can't imagine where this book would be without my amazing editor, Chris LaFontaine. He can take any of my goofily (sp?) written sentences and turn them into something beautiful. Thank you so much, my friend, for the work you've put into this book.

Third, thanks to my two poets—Jeff Larson, who wrote the opening poem and the epigraphs for each chapter, and my dear friend Melissa Anderson, who wrote the charming piece at the end of the book. Special thanks to Jeff for his unwavering support throughout the writing of this book.

Acknowledgments

And finally, thanks to my new publisher, Michael Pye, for accepting the book, and to my former publisher, Greg Brandenburgh, just for being you.

FOREWORD

I vividly and fondly remember meeting Echo Bodine for the first time many years ago at a convention in Minnesota. I knew of her and her work, so I was giddy with excitement to have the opportunity to meet her in person.

As I walked into the vendor area on the first morning of the convention, I noticed Echo standing across the room speaking to several people. Can you believe that I felt too timid to walk over and meet her? Luckily, Dave Schrader, the host of the event, approached me to say good morning, and I asked him to introduce me to Echo.

I tried my very best not to geek out when Dave made the introduction, but, despite my best efforts, I blurted out: "Oh, my God! It's Echo frickin' Bodine!" Immediately, I felt incredibly embarrassed, but Echo graciously laughed and shook my hand. My heart was racing!

I felt as if I were in the presence of royalty. And, in a manner of speaking, indeed, I was. Echo Bodine is, undisputedly, a living legend in the spiritual community. Spending time with her that weekend was pure delight. I found her to be beautiful, brilliant, and charming—a total goddess. And, as fate would have it, we became friends.

Through the years, I have been asked countless times by my clients how they can enhance their own psychic abilities. And without hesitation, I suggest that they read Echo's books *The Gift* and *A Still, Small Voice*. In my opinion, those books alone provide a master class in psychic development.

When Echo asked me to write the foreword for *How to Live A Happily Ever Afterlife*, I felt so honored and excited. In this book, she tackles a topic that troubles most of us. She attacks difficult questions like what happens after we die and what the afterlife is really like. From her own perspective, Echo shares intimate insights that she has garnered from Spirit about life after death. This book is compelling, thought-provoking, and comforting.

If you ever have the good fortune to meet (or have already met) Echo Bodine, you will agree with everything that I have said above. She is absolutely magical!

And, if you are *really* lucky, you will have the pleasure of feasting on the indescribably delicious cookies that she lovingly makes. Take it from me, they are heavenly.

I adore you, Echo frickin' Bodine!

CHIP COFFEY,
AUTHOR OF *GROWING UP PSYCHIC*

ECHOES THROUGH
THE CORRIDOR OF TIME

The lights along Lake of the Isles
Through the mist of a late October night
Remind me of an early autumn fog
Along the streets of London, a century ago.
I'm not sure how I know this, but I know
I feel it with such certainty, and see it all so clearly—
Like the large bakery windows and the scent of fresh-
baked bread
That filled the morning street on the lane where we
all lived.

Do all our thoughts and feelings ripple across time,
flowing from one century to the next?
Are we old souls with little left to learn, or young
souls thrilled to walk within this realm?
Perhaps we are or have been both, for journeys often
end where they begin.

How like the mist, how subtle is the veil, how brief
    and yet how certain is the pause
That exists between one lifetime and the next.
Do we stand with Saint Peter or Saint Paul in dis-
    tant heaven, there among the clouds,
And speak of what we learned and how we've grown,
    and then decide if we'll return again?
Or can we choose to stay in heaven's realm and join
    our voices with the song of angels?
In the shadows, in the hollow of the night, there
    among the broken and the bold,
The poets hear echoes through the corridor of time,
    and ask themselves:
Is this Lord Byron, returning to repeat the thoughts
    and feelings and actions of a writer from a far
    more gentle age?
Or is it Dylan Thomas, salt and stone, whose eyes
    reflect the darkness of the sea,
Scrolling lines immortal upon a Swansea hill as the
    sun rises slowly in the east?
And other voices ask: Have I returned to raise my
    voice again, to say, "I Have a Dream,"

Or join hands as we cross the bridge at Selma?

To rush from the boat onto the beach at Normandy,
    or plant the flag on Iwo Gima hill?

Or have I come to speak for bold Voltaire,

Who, legend says, accepted God with his dying
    breath

And so, with those few words, lying on his death bed,
    turned philosophy onto its head?

The phantom of the opera and the spirit of
    Shakespeare stand on the edge of the ending of
    time,

Whispering in each other's ears—sonnets never writ-
    ten and sad, sweet arias never sung.

Socrates is standing near; above are God and Son.

"Good night," says the sun to the moon coming on;
    "It is," says the moon to the sun.

Because fear has a dense energy to it, and they can
    take that energy in and become much taller.

"Oh, hear me," says God to his people; "We do," say
    the lovers to love.

And the guardians remain, from age unto age at the
    gates of time's vast corridor,

Echoes Through the Corridor of Time

While the passage of time helps us all realize that
photos and memories are keys.
When these moments pass and we go to look back,
we see more than those sweet memories.
It's the moments we're in and the lives we now live
that shape everything we'll ever be.

THE UPTOWN POET, JEFF LARSON
(OCTOBER 2020)

INTRODUCTION:
CROSSING THE THRESHOLD

I originally pitched this book to my publisher with the title *How to Prevent Yourself from Becoming a Ghost.* He suggested a different title: *How To Live A Happily Ever Afterlife,* noting that he thought the book was a good guide for people who didn't want to end up as lonely ghosts here on the earthly plane. I agreed.

Some souls choose to remain closer to this dimension rather than move into the light when they die. My intention here is to explain why some make that choice. To do that, I will share with you what I have learned over the last fifty-plus years of working with those whose souls have left their bodies.

When I first started to see ghosts, I had no idea what they were. I couldn't understand why these spirits, invisible to the naked eye, were hanging about in a house belonging to my mom's friend, Carol. In 1965, I was in the beginning stages of developing my psychic abilities, and I thought that ghosts looked like little white, blobby beings that floated around a room—like Casper the Friendly Ghost.

But my mom and I never did find anything even close to Casper the night we spent together in Carol's attic trying to decide what to make of the invisible people we found there. We were puzzling over an adult male and an adult female we saw there, accompanied by a son and a daughter, when we both heard a female voice in our heads saying that the woman's husband had been a smoker and an alcoholic, and that he had passed out one night with a lit cigarette and started the fire in which they had all perished.

Apparently, the entire family was hanging out in Carol's attic. Unfortunately, we had no idea what to do with them. They weren't scary-looking; they just huddled over in the corner staring at us. As silly as this sounds to me today, I had no idea at the time that ghosts were disembodied souls or that they had a human appearance. Frankly, I didn't know what a soul was, and I definitely did not understand what a ghost was.

My mother and I weren't able to give Carol any help with the tapping on the walls or the footsteps she heard every night. And it became clear to us that we still had a long way to go before we tackled another scenario like Carol's.

The Rules of the Game

The following week, we told our psychic development class about our escapade, after which our teacher, Birdie, filled us in on the dos and don'ts of ghost hunting. The first, most important piece of information she shared was not to show any fear when coming upon a ghost—at least, no visible fear. Ghosts, she said, can become more energized through others' fears, and then they can make things happen on the physical plane—knocking things off shelves, pulling clothes out of closets, making the sound of footsteps, calling out someone's name, moving the planchet on a Ouija board, or physically touching a person, to name just a few.

Birdie probably told us that ghosts were people who had passed over, but I was so freaked out by all the things she told us they could do that I don't think I heard a word after that. I've seen many ghosts since then over the span of my career, and have seen some of them literally appear to grow ten feet tall. But that always happened when I was feeling fearful. Birdie advised us to say the Lord's Prayer or a similar prayer to calm ourselves and allay our fears. She said it would also be a way of getting the ghost to return to its original size.

Finally, Birdie told us that we needed to be very firm with ghosts. They needed to look up to find a white light similar to a very full moon, she said, and go into that light. She also mentioned a tunnel that leads to that light, like a gateway to the entrance into heaven.

Another Attic, Another Ghost

Months after our experience at Carol's house, a friend of mine in the youth group at my church asked if I would come and inspect his attic for strange noises. He was hearing footsteps, banging on the walls, and chattering voices. I told him I really didn't know what I was doing, but he said that I knew more than he did, so would I please give it a try. I said I would only come if the whole youth group came with me, because I was afraid of what I might find. They all agreed to come.

As we gathered up the youth group, I told them that I needed their help. All I could remember was Birdie telling us not to be afraid. But I was definitely feeling afraid. We headed upstairs and decided to sit in a big circle *in the dark!* We held hands and waited for the spirit to show itself. Not a minute had gone by when a male spirit loomed at our circle, trying to scare all of us. I was very surprised to hear many of the group members screaming, because it meant they could see him as well. We said the Lord's Prayer out loud and watched him go from about seven feet tall down to under six feet tall. Each time we prayed, he disappeared around the corner. This back and forth routine went on for about ten minutes, with the ghost hovering over us trying to scare us, and us praying with all of our might to get him out of there.

I told the spirit firmly that he needed to leave this house and go over to the other side. And it seemed to work, because he disappeared and did not come back. The strangest part of the experience was that, when we stood up and turned on the lights, right in the middle of our big circle was a perfectly round circle of fluid.

I had heard Birdie talk about ectoplasm. She described it as a thick substance that exudes from the body of a psychic or medium to form a visible spirit, usually in a séance. But I was pretty sure it wasn't that, because ectoplasm gives off a whitish glow. To this day, I don't know what that fluid was.

When the evening was over, I told myself there would be no more of this scary stuff. I had no idea what I was doing, and I didn't want to deal with these creepy dead people.

Full House

About six years later, one of my psychic development students asked me if I would come to her house and check for ghosts. She said the house had been on the market for over a year, and that she was living in a hotel because the house appeared to be very haunted. My psychic abilities had developed quite a bit by this time, and I was trusting my visions more and more. After my experiences in Carol's attic and with my youth group, I had begun to wonder if I was making the whole thing up—just listening to my overactive imagination. It helped when others in my youth group saw that creepy guy, but I still had doubts.

So I called my younger brother, Michael, who had been psychically gifted from the time he was old enough to talk. He used to tell us about colors that appeared around people. We didn't know what these energy fields, called auras, were at the time; we just figured he had eaten too much sugar that day. When I asked him if he could see spirits, he said "yes." When I asked if they scared him, he replied "no." Then I asked if he would go with me to this student's house to see if there was a reason why the house hadn't sold in over a year. Michael said he was willing to go.

When we pulled up to the house—which was literally surrounded by a white picket fence—I couldn't imagine why someone hadn't scooped up the property. It certainly didn't look like a haunted house, or what I thought a haunted house *should* look like.

By this time in my psychic development, I was able to see and communicate with my spirit guides—the spirit helpers that we all have. So when Michael and I entered the house, we brought our guides with us.

Whoa! Holy haunted house, Batman!

With the exception of the bathrooms, every room in the house was inhabited by ghosts. I'll tell you more about this adventure in chapter 7. For now, suffice it to say that Michael and I were able to clear the entire house of ghosts. And the house sold a week later.

This night set the tone for all of our future ghost-busting jobs. Our guides walked with us through each room, pointing out things and showing us what we could do to get the spirits we found to move on into the light.

Kodak Moments

Before we go any further, I want to share three images with you. Figure 1 shows an excellent example of

Figure 1. A soul appearing as a twin of its physical body.

what a soul looks like as a twin of the physical body. Some souls can appear much bigger than their bodies, while some are about the same size. It depends on how old the soul is and the mental, emotional, and spiritual state it is in. One of the seven layers of your aura reveals your soul's energy level (see chapter 9), and a healthy aura extends out from the body anywhere from six to twelve inches. I've read that the

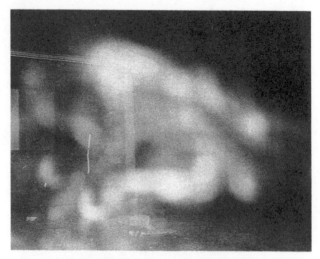

Figure 2. Five male souls dressed in blue jeans and flannel
shirts. They had all been law-enforcement officers.

aura of a healer can extend out up to thirty feet, and
that people can be healed just by standing in that
energy.

Figure 2 gives you a good example of how ghosts
can show up in photographs. I took this picture myself
several years ago, when I was participating in an episode for the television show *Sightings*. It shows five
male souls in the woods in Black Forest, Colorado.
They appear to be dressed in blue jeans and flannel
shirts. Four had been deputies; the fifth had been a

Figure 3. Police photo taken at the scene of a fatal car crash in St. Paul, Minnesota. The image appears to show the soul of a dog that had died a year before the crash.

sheriff. Ghosts rarely show up on film looking the way they look to me during a sighting.

Figure 3 is a remarkable image of a young boy who was the victim of a car crash. So far, no one has been able to give me a solid reason for why this boy's soul showed up in the photograph. The photo was taken in 1986 in St. Paul, Minnesota, at the scene of the fatal crash. The policeman who took it saw nothing unusual in the lens when he snapped the picture with his

Instamatic camera. Shortly after he turned the photos in with his report, however, the lab called him and told him that he needed to come down and see them.

The young man in the pictures was a sixteen-year-old who had been on his way to a rock concert with three friends. It was shortly after Christmas, and the roads were slippery. The car hit a patch of ice and ran into a tree. His three friends survived; he didn't. The picture seems to show that the boy is very angry about dying. If you look closely at the driver's door, you can see the soul of a dog that had belonged to the boy. But the dog had died a year before the accident. This proves—to me, at least—that animals have souls too. The boy's family never saw the picture. They didn't want to.

Media Madness

Unlike these photographic images, the way ghosts are portrayed in the popular media is often ridiculous. One of the craziest shows I've ever seen was about three men—I think they were cousins—who lived in the South. According to them, they captured a ghost in a box and took it out into the woods, where they blew it up with dynamite. I can't imagine that the show lasted more than a few episodes. Frankly, I couldn't believe that any broadcast outlet would stoop to that level.

You probably don't want to hear it, but most popular portrayals of ghosts are totally hyped for your benefit. While some may have integrity, most in the media try to scare you with demons, poltergeists, and vampires, among other creatures. But this book isn't meant to be a scary book about ghosts, goblins, and demons. It's meant to introduce you to ghosts as human beings who have chosen, through their own free will, not to move on to the place our souls call home—what religions call heaven or the afterlife. It's important to me that you learn about the human side of souls who choose to remain earth-bound for whatever reason. Sometimes they may be haunting us simply out of boredom.

The stories in this book relate actual experiences I've had, sometimes with my psychic brother,

Michael, and sometimes with students who wanted to learn how to help these souls move on to the other side. There's a point to every story and a lesson in every chapter. They are all intended to give you the "inside scoop" on why these souls chose to remain earthbound and what they needed in order to move on to a happily ever afterlife.

The added bonus will be that, if you recognize yourself in any of these stories, you still have time to heal—by changing your beliefs, by making amends, or by gaining a wider perspective about why things have happened in your life the way they have.

CHAPTER I

Who Says I'm Dead?

Change comes when it comes, like night to day.
The movement of the tide, the water's flow,
Waves upon the shore, return again into the
  endless sea.

There are two clichés we often hear about death. The first is that none of us gets out of here alive. The second is that everyone wants to go to heaven, but no one wants to go today.

These observations make sense for those of us in the land of the living. But why would *souls* choose to stay earthbound? Let's start with the least significant reason. Some souls just don't know they've died. Fortunately, this isn't common, but here are three stories that are good examples of it.

The Soldier, the Student, and the Bride

This story tells of my first encounter with a soul who claimed he did not believe he was dead. A client contacted me about a ghost who was jumping on her bed every night, trying to scare her. When she came home from work each day, she found clothes pulled out of her closet and items knocked off her dresser. She was understandably freaked out by what she was experiencing. When I first arrived at her home, I found nothing. But it wasn't long before a young man, who appeared to be in his late teens, came flying into the room.

When I first saw the ghost, whose name was Kenneth, I was definitely startled because he looked really rough—as if he had literally been through hell and back. His appearance was different from that of any ghost I had seen before. He was dressed in army fatigues and had a hole blown right through him. I had encountered many other wandering souls, but I had never before witnessed any who looked the way they did at the time of their death. I asked my guides what was going on, and they said that Kenneth did not or would not accept that he was dead. They told me that I needed to convince him in order for him to move on.

I asked Kenneth his name and why he was in this house, bothering this woman. He said he had gone off to fight in Vietnam and, when he returned, had found this woman living in his house. He told me he just wanted her to get out so he could live in peace. I could see that I definitely had my work cut out for me. I asked Kenneth what year he thought it was, and he replied that it was 1968. It was actually 1990. Kenneth was stuck in a ghostly time-warp. When I asked what his last memory was of being in Vietnam, he said he was fighting. And then he came home. I delayed as long as I could, but finally told him it was 1990 and that he had died in Vietnam.

Kenneth became really agitated and lunged at me, trying to get me to leave. I told him I wasn't leaving until I had helped him move on to the other side. He yelled that he was *not* dead and that the woman in his house was the problem, not him. This confrontation went on for close to four hours. He would leave for long periods of time, then come back and go through the whole routine with me all over again. He was clearly convinced that he was not dead. He just wanted the woman out of his house. Kenneth did eventually move on to the other side, but it took a lot of explaining to finally get him to go.

Here's another example. A student of mine committed suicide in an odd situation. She had just told her husband what she wanted for dinner and, by the time he arrived home, she was dead. Everyone was in shock at the news, because no one had suspected that she was suffering in any way. She hadn't appeared depressed, even to her closest friends. When I tuned in psychically to check on how her soul was doing, I had a vision of her standing in her kitchen, waiting for her husband to come home with dinner. I called out her name, but got no response. So I decided to wait a few days before trying to contact her again. I was certain I'd see her at her funeral, if not before, and I'd ask her then how she was doing.

I was surprised to find that the woman was *not* present at her funeral. The souls of the deceased usually wander around at their own services, taking in all that is being said about them. But she wasn't there. I tuned in while family members were giving the eulogy, and psychically checked to see where she might be. I asked the greeters on the other side if she was there. They said she wasn't. On a whim, I thought to check the last place I had found her—in her kitchen waiting for dinner. And sure enough, there she was still waiting for her husband to come home.

I could hear her thoughts. She was wondering where everyone was. Why hadn't her husband come home yet? I sent her a telepathic message asking her what she was doing. She said she was waiting for her family to come home for dinner, and that they were very, very late. I asked her what was the last thing she remembered, and she said she had spoken to her husband on the phone about dinner. Then I asked her if she had attempted to take her own life. She acted as if she didn't understand the question. I sensed a total disconnect between her actions and the reality of what had happened.

I tried to intuit words I could use to help this soul understand that she had taken her own life. The answer I got from my guides was that she needed time to come into that awareness on her own. They told me her deceased parents and brother were trying to communicate with her, but that she thought they were figments of her imagination.

I checked in on my student three months after her death, and she was still in the kitchen. When I checked in on her after another three months, she was finally gone. My guides said she was on the other side, but trying to avoid her parents. She was feeling guilty about having taken her own life.

And then there's the story of the deceased bride that I observed wandering around City Hall in St. Paul, Minnesota, when we were doing a Halloween segment for a local television station. We had received permission to investigate whether the rumors that City Hall was haunted were true. Yes, they definitely are.

The ghostly bride turned out to be a young woman who had been killed in a car accident on her way to City Hall to get married. She was pacing back and forth, frantically awaiting her fiancé. When I asked the night watchman if he was aware of her, he said that several people had seen her walking the halls in her wedding gown. I tried talking to her, but she was stuck in a scenario that played over and over in her head. She just could not accept that she was dead.

The Power of Denial

People often ask me how souls can not realize they're dead. It boils down to one simple word—*denial*. Denial is a powerful force that can lead people to declare something to be untrue, even when there is overwhelming evidence to the contrary. I can think of a few times in my own life when I have slipped into denial—refusing to acknowledge that a relationship was over when it clearly was; pretending my marriage was fine when it clearly wasn't. Oh, and my battle with alcoholism, of course. On an intuitive level,

I knew I was an alcoholic, but I kept denying it to myself and others.

Denying my true purpose and my true calling was another big denial for me. I wanted to fit in with society and have a normal career that people would accept. I suffered from the choices I was making for many years—working unsatisfying jobs, always knowing in the back of my mind that they were temporary. I knew my real work was to be a psychic and a healer. We can deny truths about ourselves and our life choices for years. So why is it so hard to see that souls might choose denial instead of moving on? Especially if they are unsure of what awaits them on the other side.

We humans can convince ourselves of pretty much anything. Think about all those who remain in bad relationships, or at jobs they hate. We tell ourselves what we want to believe. My student who killed herself did not want to own up to her actions. Many years later, she told me that she carried so much guilt about hurting her family the way she did that she stayed in denial for as long as possible.

She didn't attend her own funeral because she didn't want to see the deep grief she had caused her husband and children. She also didn't want her parents on the other side to see what she had done, so she pretended it hadn't happened. The ghostly bride in St. Paul had wanted to be married so badly that she convinced herself that her fiancé would be arriving at any moment, perpetuating the lie that she was still alive. And Kenneth simply didn't want to be dead. He wanted to live the life he had left behind him before he went to war.

If you suddenly died tomorrow, do you think you would sink into denial about it? Maybe it's something you'd rather not think about. But remember: Our goal here is to set you free from any of the emotional entanglements that might keep you earthbound. Are there entanglements in your life that might lead you to deny your own death? Would you have a hard time accepting your own death if you were to die suddenly? Do you think you are the kind of person who might deny death in order to remain a ghost here on the earthly plane?

~ *Exercise* ~

Look back over your life and see where you may have chosen denial instead of looking at what was really happening in your world. Note everything that comes to mind about experiences you denied were happening. Write those things down, then write down how you eventually recognized your denial and what you did to move past it.

CHAPTER 2

Home Is Where the Heart Is

Sunshine upon the fields of life, dissolves routine like sun upon the snow.
The red thread flows from one lifetime to the next.

The second reason souls may choose to remain earth-bound is that they simply don't like change. When my brother and I go into a haunted home or business, the first thing we do is establish who and what we're dealing with. We visit each room, checking for a transparent form. These apparitions look just like the living, except that they have a kind of graying energy and a somewhat haggard look. We ask their names and why they want to stay where they are. With the exception of a Mr. Peterson we once encountered, they all offer us their first name only. Then they explain why they are there.

It's simple: They don't like change. They don't want to move on. They want to stay where they are and continue to do the work and live the lives that made them happy when they were alive.

We all get stuck in patterns. Having routines is part of being human. Those routines help keep us grounded, help us move through our day. They help us think better—or so it seems. But sometimes these patterns become fixed in our lives and we never change them. That is not growth. That is being stuck. And that's what these ghosts are. Stuck.

Here are three stories about souls I have encountered who were definitely stuck on the wrong side of the threshold.

The Undertaker, the Policeman, and the Teacher

I once met the ghost of a very nice gentleman who ran a funeral parlor when he was alive. He believed he was still doing that same work. No, he said, he did not want to move on, and he didn't want to try anything new. He was happy where he was. The problem was that everyone kept hearing noises coming from his basement workshop, and it was scaring the people who worked there. He told me that he would stop making the noises, but did not want to move on. This was all he knew and he wanted to continue doing it.

Another soul who was stuck here was a policeman named Bob. Bob told me that he had protected the girls at a massage parlor when he was living, and continued to protect them now that he was deceased. He did not want to move on. He had been protecting the girls for years, and did not want to change. The problem was that he scared the ladies one Saturday night when he pulled a shower curtain off the wall. The girls had gotten used to the banging on the walls, but the shower curtain was a whole other level of fright for them.

Bob told me that banging on the walls was his way of protecting the girls. If one of them had a bad client, he would make a noise to warn them that the person wasn't trustworthy. He said the shower curtain incident was quite different. He had been angry about the person in the shower and acted out of rage. The owner of the parlor later told me that the customer was a priest. Who knows? Maybe Bob didn't like the thought of a priest going to a massage parlor. I suggested to Bob that he move on and begin a new life on the other side. He said he preferred the life he had, and he did not want to change.

And then there was the high school teacher whom I met one evening after the school's principal called me for help. Students were seeing her walk the halls, and it was freaking them out. The teacher had died of cancer a few months before and was actually pulling people's hair or touching them on the shoulder as she wandered the halls. It took me a while to locate her, and, in the process, we found a lot of other ghosts in the school. Some were young people who had died but chose to hang out at the school with the living. They did not want to move on either. When I asked the teacher why she didn't want to go into the light, she told me that the students needed her. When I asked my spirit guides about it, they said that she did not want to change. She wanted to continue with her daily routine because it was all she knew and all she wanted to know.

Here We Go Around Again

Do you ever wonder about everything we go through here in this life and what the purpose of our experiences might be? Do you ever wonder why souls are created in the first place? Or why they come to this earthly plane to begin with? I'm a very curious Virgo who loves to analyze everything that happens, and this is something I have studied and researched for my whole life. And my questions have led me to a firm belief in reincarnation.

When I was first introduced to the idea of reincarnation, I thought only pot-smoking hippies believed in it. It was the 1960s, and many young people were talking about the Age of Aquarius and other "woo woo" New Age stuff. My teacher at the time, a Spiritualist minister, definitely believed in it. When she taught us the reasoning behind reincarnation, it led me to try past-life regression and to read several books on the subject.

That research, as well as the many past-life readings I've done for clients over the years, has left no doubt in my mind that reincarnation is real. And knowing this has changed my relationship with God completely. When you realize the reason for all your lifetimes, you discover that God is not some villain in the sky who causes bad things to happen to you in your life. You realize that one important purpose of having several lifetimes is to grow.

When our souls are first created, we are like babies. We haven't developed much consciousness about anything yet. We come into this world to grow, and to develop an understanding about everything we experience here. That takes quite a few lifetimes. And we develop both good and bad patterns along the way through our actions. These patterns, taken collectively, constitute what's called our "karma" (see chapter 9). If we don't make amends or balance out that karma at some point, we come back again and again to resolve and release these patterns (see chapter 3). This process has no time line. We have all eternity to work things out, to grow, and to become more and more enlightened. When our souls reach a certain level of awareness and development, we no longer need to come back to the earthly plane. Thus we actually do create our own realities based on our consciousness.

The families we are born into, or adopted into, are an important part of our life's plan. Our parents and siblings provide the framework for the experiences we come here to work through. Some families have been torn apart because of differing views and beliefs. But why would we be put into a family whose views differ radically from ours? It's simple. To learn from each other. To understand why each family member believes the way they do. It takes a lot of growth to accommodate the views of others and to learn from them.

We are all constantly growing—or perhaps I should say that we are all *supposed* to be constantly growing. The stories above tell of ghosts who refused to grow. But souls that resist growth are missing the experiences they need to have and the lessons they need to learn for their own evolution. Because of free will, they can choose not to live according to their life's plan. But it's uncomfortable when you're not living the path you were meant to live. Unfortunately, some souls get used to that anguished feeling and refuse to move on.

So how do you react to change? Are you someone who does the same thing day after day, week after week, month after month, with very little change to your routine? Do you get anxious when something throws off your schedule? Do you hyper-ventilate at the thought of trying something new? If you answered "yes" to any of these questions, how do you think you will handle death?

~ Exercise ~

Take some time right now to answer the questions above. Be honest with yourself and write down your answers. No one else will see what you write unless you choose to share it with them. It's important to become aware of patterns that you may have established a long time ago. Do you literally do the same thing day after day? Do you eat the same food? Take the same route to work? Go to the same stores? Play the same way you have for years?

Many years ago, my minister gave a sermon on the importance of changing our routines. You could hear people in the congregation groaning. He said that when we don't allow change into our lives, we become like robots, living on automatic pilot. When this happens, he said, we're not really living. We're just existing.

Think of simple things you can change in your life—like whether you brush your teeth before or after you shower. Change up your routine in small ways and see if you start to come alive again. Take a different route to work. Go to a different grocery store. Change the shoes you wear every day. Practicing with small changes will make larger changes easier to accept.

CHAPTER 3

Nice to See You–Or Not

Questions are answered, doubts resolved,
When we look upon it all through the eyes of God.

The third reason why souls choose to remain earth-bound is to avoid seeing someone on the other side. They may not want to run into someone who was abusive toward them, or perhaps someone they may have harmed. In fact, there are many reasons why souls may feel uncomfortable meeting someone they once knew.

Souls like these would rather take up residence almost anywhere else to avoid running into someone from their past who now resides on the other side.

We have a long list of places where we have found these ghosts—a tanning parlor, a treatment center, a nursing home, a hospital, a business, a grocery store, and a stranger's attic, basement, or shower. (I've always wondered why showers are such popular places for ghosts to hang out.) And the list of souls these ghosts wanted to avoid is equally long—lovers, family, friends, neighbors, and business associates. Here are a few examples of souls who chose to stay earthbound so they wouldn't run in to those they wanted to avoid on the other side.

Lovers, Family, and Friends

Sherry's boyfriend killed her and then committed suicide. She told me there was no way she ever wanted to see him again, which is understandable. Robert had cheated on his wife throughout their marriage. After his wife died from cancer, he feared she might have found out about the affairs once she got to the other side. So when he died, he chose to stay right here.

John, a young man who hung himself in an elevator shaft, told us he did not want to see his parents on the other side. He was too ashamed that he had taken his own life. And sweet little Eva, whom I saw standing in the window of an old, abandoned house, said she didn't want to go to heaven because she didn't want to see a sister who had been very mean to her. Katherine had abandoned her children and did not want to encounter any of them on the other side. Another man committed suicide after he had stolen a great deal of money from friends. He did not want to run into any of them on the other side either.

First, let me state the obvious—at least to me. Heaven is a huge place. Enormous. Moreover, it is an expansive and healing place. The chances of running into souls we want to avoid there are very slim. When we first die, our souls come out of the body and normally head straight into the white light. Each soul is bigger and brighter than a full moon, so there's little chance of it not being seen. Usually, a family member or a friend comes to greet each soul, showing it the way into the light. We do have free will, however, and we can continue to exert that free will after we pass. So we can indeed choose to remain earthbound.

Forgive and Forget

Chances are, the souls who choose to stay here are those souls who have not developed much consciousness. I describe them as being at the first level in their soul's development (see chapter 4). They have no interest in other people or animals unless it benefits them. They are often labeled narcissistic, and they like portraying themselves as powerful. They haven't developed compassion yet, which is important for all of us. In fact, they are in the very first stages of their soul's growth. Unfortunately, choosing to remain earthbound can stifle their growth even more.

Souls who do not want to run into someone on the other side—like Sherry, John, Robert, or Katherine—are doing themselves a disservice. When we experience negative emotions like guilt, shame, hatred, resentment, rage, and fear, we can doom ourselves to remain stuck for a very long time. Many of us have experienced painful relationships with abusive spouses, or dysfunctional families, or nasty neighbors, or terrible bosses while we were alive. Long after these relationships are over, we can still be very affected by them. And that means that, even in death, we can still be haunted by them.

And here's something that's very important to understand about the people in your life. Anyone who is more than a casual acquaintance in this life is almost certainly someone from one of your previous lives. In fact, the more significant others are to you now, the more involved you were with them in past lives. Your relationships change from lifetime to lifetime. Your mom in this lifetime may have been a sister, a brother, a husband or wife, a child or grandparent, a boss, or a neighbor in one of your previous lives.

We come into this life accompanied by people who will be either our allies or our foes, and each one of them has a purpose for being there. Indeed, our relationships are one of the biggest learning tools we have. They strengthen or weaken us, support or deny us, love or dislike us. Our souls recognize our former relationships, and that's why we may immediately feel drawn to someone we meet. But we may also become uneasy, feeling as if we need to watch our backs. There's so much we can learn from the relationships we experience in our lifetimes. And that's exactly how it is supposed to be. Some are with us for a short time; others may be with us for an entire lifetime—or more.

Because of this, I can't stress enough the importance of looking at your relationships and making amends when you've hurt others. And it's equally important to forgive the pain others have caused you—that's the tough part. Your pride and ego can get wrapped up in feelings of fairness versus feelings of injustice, and you can stay stuck for lifetimes. At some point, you have to look at your circumstances from a higher perspective. You need to see what is required in order to break the dysfunctional patterns you've created. You need to resolve your karma.

Souls like Eva are stuck feeling like victims. These kinds of relationships are far more common among underdeveloped souls than they are with those who have learned to look at life from a higher perspective. Was there a person in your life who hurt you or made you feel guilty or ashamed? What did that person teach you about yourself? Perhaps that person's purpose in your life was to teach you something about your life's plan. Did that lesson help you grow? Can you see how the relationships in your life have enriched it, including the dysfunctional ones?

We are often told to "look at life through God's eyes." We are all striving to get to a level of development where we can see the higher purpose for all we have been through. We all want to leave the roles of victim or victimizer behind. When we can look at life from this higher perspective—physically, mentally, emotionally, and spiritually—we no longer see things from a limited, human point of view.

Here's an example. Let's say you were raised by a self-centered, alcoholic mother who had very little time for you. Your life revolved around her needs, not yours. Did you grow up totally codependent, believing that people loved you only if you lost touch with yourself and focused on their needs rather than your own? Or did you learn to fight for yourself, knowing that your needs and wants were just as important, and that being codependent is not the way to gain love?

A life like this may have been difficult, but it may also have become one of the most rewarding lives you've ever lived because it taught you to see things from a higher perspective. Every day, you have a choice. Are you going to be the victim or the victor? The victor looks at all of the positives that come out of every experience, and grows by leaps and bounds. The victim stays stuck, getting victimized over and over again—and never grows.

Making Amends

When you think about people with whom you have had relationships in your life but who are now living on the other side, what names come to you that are connected with unresolved emotional issues? Do feel a stab in your heart when you think of them or hear their names? Remember: every significant person in your life is there for a reason. Depending on how self-aware you are, you may have noticed a certain feeling inside you when you first met someone. That was your soul reacting either favorably or cautiously.

Our souls recognize our friends and foes from previous lives, but we may not be conscious of what our feelings about them are—which, in most cases, is a good thing. Otherwise, it might be extremely confusing to deal with the relationships in our current life as well as all the feelings we harbor about them from previous lives. When I saw my ex-husband for the first time, I became almost obsessed with marrying him. I knew I had to marry him and I didn't want to waste any time. I couldn't explain to anyone why I felt this was so imperative—including myself. We wed two months after meeting, and the relationship only lasted for a little over a year. But my soul accomplished a great deal in that short time. I'm so grateful that I've taken the time to deal with all the emotions left over from that relationship, because I know that if I hadn't, it would have been difficult for me to meet him on the other side. The same was true for me with my dad.

Just because people with whom we have emotional baggage die does not mean that the pain involved in the relationship goes away. They may have created or perpetuated patterns with which we are still living, and these may be destructive patterns. It would be so nice if we all made clean breaks from our relationships when they ended, but we don't. And old pain can linger forever.

I seriously doubt that you bought this book to guide you through therapy sessions with yourself. But I am serious when I say that I don't want you to end up a lonely ghost roaming the earthly plane for fear of having to confront previous relationships. Is there anyone in your life, dead or alive, with whom you still have unfinished business? Anyone who could keep you from moving on to heaven when you pass?

Is there anyone with whom you had a problem that was never resolved—anyone you would be uncomfortable meeting on the other side? Don't just quickly say "no" and then move on. Take as much time with these questions as you need to. If necessary, step back and then return to them later, because the answers are important for you. Somewhere along the line, people got the idea that, once we die, all of these unresolved emotional memories just go away, but they don't. They stay with us until they are healed.

The best part about healing these wounds is that it enables you to see why these relationships went the way they did. When you discover what the original intention of the relationship was and what it was there to help you accomplish, you learn to see it from a higher perspective. I'm very familiar with all the "yeah buts" we tend to fall back on. And I know that making amends—admitting that we hurt someone—can be very humbling. But it's also very liberating, and that's what we're striving for. Resolving our pain, our past mistakes, our regrets, our shame and guilt—making amends to those we've hurt and accepting their amends, should they offer them—gives us exactly the freedom our souls seek. I guarantee you that there's nothing better than going home with a clean slate.

Making amends is one of the most important things we can do in our lifetimes! You don't want to have unfinished business when you pass away, because you take all that baggage with you. Emotions are energy, and that energy can sit stored away in your soul for lifetimes. If you don't deal with it on this side, or on the other side between lifetimes, you bring it back with you in a future life. Because your soul needs to heal.

~ Exercise ~

Make a list of any and all unresolved emotional issues still lingering for you. Write them out in detail. Be specific about what happened. Note how those emotions left you feeling, and what you would like to do about them now. What do you you need to do in order to let them go?

When you are done with that list, write out a list of the people you've hurt, whether intentionally or not. Be honest with yourself about why the relationship went the way it did, and what you would like to do today to make amends. How would you feel if you died today and ran into these souls in heaven? Our egos like to kid themselves that they have no unfinished business here, but if you give this enough thought, you almost certainly will come up with one or two names.

If you're having a hard time remembering, ask God or the universe to remind you of any negative energy you're holding in your body, your mind, or your soul that you don't want to carry with you when you pass. I hate the thought of having to "ghostbust" you some-day, just because there are people in heaven you don't want to see. Come on, wipe the slate clean. Don't have regrets when you pass. March over to the other side with a big smile on your face, ready to see anyone from your previous lives. Doesn't that sound nice?

Of course, you can wait to get clear of all of this baggage on the other side, so if you'd rather bring it with you, that's your prerogative. But isn't it nice that we have choices?

CHAPTER 4

Fear of Flying

Across the world wide, beyond the great divide,
Seek to understand, reach from darkness into light.

The fourth reason why souls have not moved on to the other side is that they believe that there is *nothing* after death. No heaven, no hell, no God, no nothing. They believe that they will no longer exist after death, so they choose instead to hang out in a place called the "astral plane"—a dimension between our earthly plane and the other side. Thousands of souls are stuck there, and most are not very pleasant. They all seem to have a chip on their shoulders; they all seem to be mad at the world. They spent their whole lives denouncing any kind of afterlife or God, and this puts them in a bind. They obviously continue to exist. It's just that their egos don't want to acknowledge it.

I have talked to some of these souls, and it's always such an odd conversation. When I ask them why they haven't moved on, they tell me that there is no such thing as life after death. So, I ask, how is it that I am able to have a conversation with them if they no longer exist? At that point, they usually float away from me, because they don't want to engage anymore. They often appear angry, egotistical, and bullish. It's as if there's no beginning or ending for them.

These spirits roam the astral plane trying to figure this all out. They often become the souls or ghosts who communicate through Ouija Boards and play tricks on people. They scare children, knock things off shelves, and generally cause a ruckus wherever they go. Personally, I don't think all of these souls (mainly men) are demons or evil spirits. But the astral plane is definitely where such spirits exist, and it's their egos that keep them there. They have no desire to admit they were wrong.

This chapter and the next one were difficult to write because they deal with sensitive material—demons, possession, evil spirits, and such. Moreover, I know that some people will read them and decide that everything I describe here is happening to them. People tend to gravitate toward negativity, fear, and drama. Although I hate to create more of these feelings, I can't simply ignore these topics. So, if you are someone who reads about the side-effects of a drug and then thinks you are experiencing all of them, I want you to keep this in mind as you read on.

Ghost Writer

In 1965, my mom and I were told by a medium in Minnesota that she, my brother, Michael, and myself would all become well-known psychics someday. We didn't have a clue what that meant. Against the advice of our psychic teacher, Birdie, we bought a Ouija Board and enough incense to last a lifetime. Birdie warned us that ghosts and spirits could work through the board. She said that, although they would communicate positively in the beginning, after a while, they would turn to negative messages. She told us that we should be able to see who was reaching out to us through the board and warned us that even if they told us they were our spirit guides, chances are they were not. Birdie certainly knew what she was talking about.

Using the Ouija Board was fun in the beginning. We were curious, watching with great interest as the planchet moved across the board spelling out messages from the world beyond. Then all kinds of strange things started happening in our home. Every night when we were eating dinner, we could all hear the sounds of a typewriter typing. When we went upstairs to my bedroom to see if the sounds were coming from my typewriter, they stopped, and we were never able to tell where or how the typing noises were being made.

One night, besides the sounds of typing, we heard strange-sounding voices calling my name. My mother immediately called Birdie, who asked if we had a

Ouija Board in my closet. My mother answered "yes." Birdie said that several disincarnate souls (ghosts) had attached themselves to the board and wanted us to come and play. She told my mother to burn the board in the fireplace and never to buy another one, explaining that these souls had nothing better to do than scare young girls at slumber parties—something that frequently happened to me as a young girl. We had grown so fond of the board, however, that we just couldn't burn it. So we took it outside and put it in the garbage. The next morning, when we came downstairs for breakfast, we found the board on the kitchen table. Then we burned it.

There had been so many odd disturbances in our home. Things were moved or went missing. Strange sounds echoed through the house—banging on walls and footsteps. And we always had the feeling that we were being watched. From the time we brought the board into the house, the house always had a creepy vibe. After we burned it to ashes, however, the disturbances started to diminish. I have never forgotten what Birdie told us. If we couldn't see who was actually working the board, we should stay away from it completely. She was so right.

Since then, when we've been called to clear a haunted house, we often find that someone has brought a Ouija Board into the home, and that, shortly thereafter, things began to happen. Spirits who have little consciousness about anything begin to make their presence known. Most people are too embarrassed to admit that they have a Ouija Board, so they pretend all of these little happenings are just coincidences.

If you are a skeptic who is looking for proof that spirits exist, don't bring a Ouija Board into your home. These spirits love to mess with your head. If they claim to be Jesus, or one of the Archangels, or some other wise being trying to bring you a "very important message," don't get sucked in. I don't know much about Archangels, but I do know that they've got way more important work to do than play with a game board.

The astral world is full of souls who get bored. They want to stir up trouble. If you feel you may have one or more of these souls in your home, be very authoritative and demand that they leave. Treat them as you would any other intruder who might come into your space. Don't stand for it.

Almost Heaven

Another category of ghosts found in the astral plane are souls who believe in a place that Catholics call purgatory—a place where souls go to be purified so they can enter heaven. Different religions have differing beliefs about places like purgatory. My experience is that it's a dark, empty void where souls wander around, waiting to be told that they are done suffering and can go on to heaven. Many of these souls are good Catholics who are committed to suffering as long as necessary if it means that they can eventually meet God or Jesus.

There are many different beliefs about how we pass from life into death. Most Christians believe they die only once and that, after death, if their spirits are judged worthy, they then exist in an afterlife for all eternity. Buddhists, on the other hand, believe that upon death, they are reborn into another life. Hindus believe that the afterlife consists of a span of time spent in a heaven or hell, depending on the karma they have built up in this life. Muslims believe death is the cessation of biological life, after which the spirit rests in the grave until Judgment Day. Traditional Jews believe that immortality brings the resurrection of the body and soul, followed by God judging the worthiness of their lives. An afterlife is an essential part of the Mormon faith as well, while Native American cultures hold various beliefs about life after death.

The image I have of passing from life into whatever comes after includes the astral plane, which I see as a very busy place with thousands of souls who wander there without a clear idea of why. I believe that the demons and evil spirits that some encounter in this life reside in this purgatory-like place. They are angry. They feel victimized by life; they have very little, if any, consciousness. They only care about themselves. In short, I see the astral plane as a creepy, unpleasant place inhabited by unhappy and sometimes miserable souls who should move on into the light and leave the living alone.

Buck and the Bouncer

One such spirit was named Buck. My encounter with Buck in a Kentucky bar was featured on a segment I did for the A&E network several years ago. Some ghosts are mean and nasty—definitely of lower consciousness—and Buck fits that description to a T.

I had been to this particular bar twice before for different television shows (see chapter 5). This third visit was intended to follow up on these previous encounters and see if things were just as crazy as they had been the first time I went there. In fact, the situation had escalated. When I first arrived, the bouncer told me that he had been hit over the head with a beer bottle, resulting in a wound that required twenty-one stitches. He thought he had been attacked by Alonso, one of the ghosts I had met on my first visit. But it wasn't Alonso at all.

After our initial greetings, the bouncer went and sat down at the bar while I walked around looking for the ghost who had hit him with the bottle. I distinctly remember coming around the corner and literally "bumping" into a spirit who appeared to be almost ten feet tall. The shock of the encounter took my breath away for a second or two. Then I asked the spirit his name and why he was there. He said that his name was Buck, and that he was a friend of the owner. Apparently, Buck had killed his own brother and died shortly after getting out of prison. He didn't know where to go because he didn't believe in life after death, so he came to his friend's bar. He gave off a powerful, angry, and hateful energy.

I asked Buck if he was the one who had hit the bouncer with the beer bottle, and he said that he was. Then I asked him how he had done it, because it's not easy for a spirit to pick up any kind of material object. Buck told me to watch and he would show me. He floated over and put his mouth right up to the bouncer's mouth. Then he breathed in the bouncer's energy. Right before my eyes, the bouncer's head went down on the bar and he fell fast asleep. I asked the bartender how often this happened and he said almost every night.

This angry, hateful spirit was taking the bouncer's energy, which gave him the power to make physical phenomena happen around the bar. I told Buck that I thought what he was doing was terrible, and that he should leave the poor guy alone. He told me to go to hell.

When the bouncer woke up, I told him he should yell at the spirit whenever he started feeling as if someone were draining his energy. He told me he just couldn't because he was too afraid of what the ghost might do to him.

The Power of Fear

Ghosts are made up of energy, and the more energy we give them, the more they are able to do. We give them that energy through our fear. The bouncer who was hit by Buck walked around projecting fear all day long, and that was a constant source of energy for Buck.

I can easily see people assuming that Buck was a demon because he looked so angry and had a cold, uncaring energy. In fact, thousands of people believe in demons, but I don't have a lot to say about them. In the last thirty-plus years as a ghostbuster, I've never even seen one! I know there are many psychics who swear that demons exist, and I'm not going to say they are wrong. I'm just saying that I've never seen any. I've seen mean, crabby, hateful, aggressive ghosts, but they have all been the souls of former people who haven't appeared demonic to me in any way.

When I was younger—in my twenties and thirties, and learning about all of this—I often saw normal-looking ghosts (souls) turn themselves into something that looked like demonic creatures, but when I yelled at them or said a prayer, they just turned back into regular ghosts. These ghosts sometimes generated fear by scratching people, or hitting them, or pushing them. Sometimes they even appeared as grotesque monsters. But in the end, they were just the souls of others who simply wanted to be like that. I do believe in possession, however. But the souls I have seen who possess others are usually addicts of some kind (see chapter 5).

Several people have called us over the years claiming that they have a demon or an evil spirit in their home. What we have always found when we investigated, however, were just very hateful, angry ghosts. The people were living in fear of these spirits, who believed that they were stronger than any kind of higher power. And that fear continued to "feed the monster."

Think about going to a haunted house. People walk around scared to death thinking that every strange sound they hear or every flicker of a light they see is a ghost. And all that fear just feeds the ghosts who live there. The homes we visit generally start out with small annoyances that soon turn into bigger ones. In fact, it's the fear of the people who live there that makes it possible for the ghosts to do more physically.

Evil Spirits

To me, evil spirits fit into the same category as demons. The distinction generally made between the two is that demons are blobs of very negative energy coming from the devil, while evil spirits are the souls of former people with an axe to grind. It seems as if a high percentage of television shows and movies these days are all about evil. Evil, evil, evil. But I know that people's minds are strong enough to conjure up just about anything. And I've seen regular ghosts turn devilish or evil in appearance just to frighten people and feel more powerful.

Religion has supported the concept of evil for centuries through teachings that are damaging to our souls. Moreover, TV has a way of making evil look cool—handsome, beautiful, powerful, and wealthy. But being evil is inhuman. The reality is that evil is driven by the need for power. And the drive to acquire power over others can only succeed when those individuals feel powerless. Think about the bullies you encountered in school. They often had difficult home lives or were abused in one way or another. They felt powerless to do anything about their situation, so they went down the dark path of nastiness to make others fearful of them. Life will come crashing down on people like this at some point, however, and they will eventually come face to face with their lack of power. I see these spirits as young souls who are trying to convince people that they're evil. They thrive on the fear we project.

I see "evil spirits" as deceased bullies, however, not as demons who cause horrible things to happen. Many choose to believe that Satan is to blame for their bad behavior, because that falls in line with their beliefs that there are demons and evil spirits who try to interfere with our lives. But I can't conceive of anything being more powerful than God. I know there's a lot going on out there that I don't know about. But since I'm writing this book to share my experiences with you, I can only tell you what I have learned. The energies that pretend to be evil spirits and demons are just souls who are stuck on the astral plane and incapable of moving on. Their fate can change, however, when they become willing to grow.

Soul Levels

So how did these evil or demonic souls get that way? Why are these poor souls the way they are?

Well, it has to do with something I call "soul levels." As I explain in my book *Echoes of the Soul*, souls exist at four different levels of development. Level 1 souls are totally self-absorbed. Level 2 souls have begun to open their hearts to others. Level 3 souls have continued to grow and learn. Level 4 souls have reached a point in their development where they strive to understand their oneness with all living beings. Let's look at each of these levels separately and then examine how they act as a vehicle for soul development.

Level 1 souls are completely unaware that there is a connection among all living things. They are totally focused on their own survival. They live in fear. And because they believe there is never enough to go around, they take whatever they want. These souls ignore the inner voice that tells us all right from wrong. They live as if this is their only life and that the law of karma does not apply to them. They feel completely disconnected from everyone else and do not believe in a power greater than themselves. Thus they have not begun to love in the greater sense. They treat people, animals, and nature without respect, selfishly taking whatever they want for their own gratification, without any concern for others. It is at this level that a soul's karma begins. Level 1 souls have very little consciousness. They are just starting out on their journey of growth and are just beginning to develop an emotional awareness.

The universe contains many solar systems, and even more planets within those systems. I believe that our souls go to different planets to learn different things. Earth is considered an emotional planet, so we come here to experience emotion and learn from it.

Robert Plutchik enumerates eight basic human emotions:

- Fear—feeling anxiety, mistrust, dread, or terror
- Anger—feeling fury, resentment, or rage
- Sadness—feeling sorrow, grief, or loss (for example, when someone has died)
- Joy—feeling happiness, delight, or gladness
- Disgust—feeling revulsion, aversion, or loathing
- Surprise—feeling astonishment, wonder, or shock
- Trust—feeling confidence or belief in something, or a commitment to something
- Anticipation—feeling hope, expectation, or looking forward positively to something

Most of us hate experiencing strong emotions because they make us feel vulnerable. But when we allow ourselves to feel emotions, we eventually learn to master them.

Souls at Level 2 are less self-absorbed and less fearful than Level 1 souls, yet most of the time they still live in a state of fear. They are slowly opening up to the possibility that they are not completely alone, however, and they are learning to stop seeing others as unimportant or as threats to their own survival. They cautiously begin to reach out to people and animals, and begin to appreciate the natural world around them. These souls have learned a lot, but they sometimes can revert to Level 1 if they don't pay careful attention to the lessons they learn in life.

Level 2 souls are kind of "getting it." They may still be struggling with the roles of victim or victimizer, but they are learning to connect with people, animals, and nature. They are beginning to get a glimpse of kindness and caring. Both Level 1 and Level 2 souls have usually led hard lives. They may have been raised in families that belonged to strict religions. They may have heard a lot about fire and brimstone, and been taught to fear Satan. These lessons have left them feeling so powerless that they pursue evil and power in any form they can. Gangs and gun violence reflect this desire to feel powerful. In our work with souls stuck in the astral plane, we have encountered many nasty ghosts. They are definitely all Level 1 and Level 2 souls.

Level 3 souls have begun to understand and remember more of their oneness with all humanity and their connection to God. At Level 3, souls connect to God through their religion or their faith. These souls tend to see God as an agent of shame and punishment, however. They alternate between fear of survival, fear of others, and fear of God, and, in the process, they begin to learn to trust. Level 3 souls take their first tentative steps in a positive direction when they start to move away from their self-absorbed, fearful states into broader and more inclusive belief systems. As they do, they stop focusing on how and why they are separate from others and discover the similarities that link all of humanity.

Level 4 souls have discovered and appreciate the oneness of all living beings—animal and human—with God, and they try to live their lives accordingly. After having spent many difficult lifetimes learning the lessons of Levels 1, 2, and 3, they are now searching for a greater understanding about all of life. They ask more questions and read more books. They have embarked on their spiritual quest. Those with addictions from previous lives usually recover from them when they reach Level 4.

This level is about healing all that has taken place on the soul's journey through the first three levels. We need to heal our souls in order to move on to the other side fully and stay there. We can easily spend fifty lifetimes at each of the four levels, learning everything we can from life on Earth. It's not a quick process by any means. Fortunately, our reactions to emotions change over time. Most of us have probably felt and acted like victims in emotional situations at one time or another. Our goal, however, is to stop seeing and feeling ourselves as victims and learn to see the good in each of life's experiences and grow from them. This learning can take lifetimes because of the soul's resistance to feeling vulnerable. We can get stuck in these patterns. That's why it's so important to take an inventory of your beliefs from time to time.

Stepping Up

Twelve-step recovery programs can be phenomenal tools for your soul's development. In most of these programs, the tenth step is about taking a daily inventory of your thoughts, actions, and feelings. And this is key to your soul's growth. The eighth and ninth steps entail making a list of those you've harmed, and this can also be incredibly valuable when it comes to soul development.

Remember all of those ghosts who were afraid to go to the other side because they didn't want to have to face someone there? If you take care of these issues in this life, you won't feel a need to avoid others when you cross over. If you've got your ducks in a row, so to speak, when your physical death occurs, you can cross that threshold with no worries about unfinished business. That's one of great secrets of living a happily ever afterlife.

The thing about evil spirits—those stuck here on the earthly plane for one reason or another who show malign intent—is that they had to have been evil people when they were living. Now, when I think of evil people, I think of people like Adolf Hitler, who ordered the killing of millions of Jews, or Saddam Hussein, the dictator who killed thousands of his people because they "didn't fall in line." Or

Josef Mengele, who performed deadly experiments on prisoners in Auschwitz. Or Pol Pot, dictator of Cambodia who killed 300,000 innocents. Or Joseph Stalin, who murdered a million of his own citizens because they would not accept his oppressive regime. To me, this is evil. But in the fifty-plus years I've been doing this work, I've never seen an evil ghost who bore any resemblance to any of these monsters.

Of course, we all probably have our own definitions of evil. When I look up the word in my Thesaurus, I find synonyms like wickeness, depravity, corruption, immorality, perversity, malevolence, indecency, hatred, and viciousness. Now, I can believe in evil spirits more easily than I can believe in demons because I know that there are many evil people here on Earth who fit these descriptions and who may try to harm the living. But how sad it is to think that these souls have carried their evil intentions over into death.

There are many communities on the other side, each one reflecting a different reality and purpose. When I asked my guides what happened to Saddam

Hussein when he died, they showed me a community of dictators like himself who all lived together. I can't even begin to picture what that would be like, with all those evil egos arguing that their way is the best way.

Western religions largely ignore the principle of karma—the belief that we are all responsible for our actions toward others. They teach about the Golden Rule, but don't explain that it's imperative that we treat others as we want to be treated because the law of karma means that we get back what we send out. They make the principle sound like a suggestion— like telling us that we reap what we sow. In fact, all the negativity in the world stands as proof that this principle is not truly taken to heart. Instead of talking about karma, Western religions try scaring us with the devil and fire and brimstone. And it is in that fear of going to hell that younger souls get stuck at the lower levels of development. They learn not to question what they've been taught, and they accept teachings on punishment as "gospel truth."

The good news is that eventually souls step up from Levels 1 and 2 to Levels 3 and 4. They start to move away from restrictive religious beliefs and begin to explore more inclusive faiths. When this happens, Level 4 souls move into a spirituality that is more broadly based than dogmatic religions, and seek a personal understanding of the universe and what makes it tick. They want to know who or what God is. They no longer buy into a belief in hell or purgatory as a place of punishment and retribution.

Souls who step out of these belief systems realize how important it is to heal their old beliefs and the hurt those beliefs have caused. They step onto a path that leads to healing victims from within, and learning about the false sense of power. They begin to understand the difference between man's will and ego, and the will of God. And they recognize the feminine side of God while discovering the divine part of themselves. This connection is made by listening to the still small voice within, the voice of the Creator. When souls step up in this way, they go from having no consciousness to enjoying complete consciousness.

When souls have learned everything they can from their experiences on the earthly plane, they release their karma and can move on to the other side for good. They only return to Earth if they want to be helpful. Have you ever met someone that you would call an "Earth Angel"—someone who has no karma left to work through? If so, you probably experienced them as loving, almost magical souls who had a certain glow about them. Yes, they're here. And they come to help us heal our souls on all levels.

~ Exercise ~

This is actually more of a warning than an exercise.

Try asking yourself these questions. What are your beliefs about demons? What do you think they look like? What do you believe they are capable of doing? Do you live in fear of demons? Do you wish you could see one? Do you believe they come from hell or worship Satan? Do you think you will be an evil spirit when you die?

I know there are many out there who think it might be cool to be demonic or evil in death and to scare people. All I can say to them is to repeat that famous one liner: "Payback is a bitch." The law of karma requires that whatever we do to others comes back to us—and that includes all the good we do for others. It's so much nicer to have good karma reflected back to us than nasty bad karma.

There is another universal law that says "like attracts like." That means that you will attract spirits and people who believe the same way you do. If you study demonology and want to hang out with demons or have a strong belief in evil, your chances of attracting these kinds of spirits to you are higher than they are for the average person who is just curious about them. I hope you'll reconsider wanting to attract these souls to you, because there is absolutely no pay-off in it for you.

CHAPTER 5

Give Me More!

Peer through the looking glass, unto the other side.
Hold fast until the darkness fades, then walk into the
light.

As we've seen, there are many reasons why some souls remain earthbound—denying that they're dead, resistance to change, and fear of what lies beyond life. But every time I witness this next reason, it really creeps me out. I'm speaking about the souls of those who suffered from an addiction of some sort in life—alcohol, drugs, food, or sex—and they want more!

These souls don't want to accept that they are deceased simply because they are still trying to meet the needs of their addiction. They do this by finding someone living who has the same addiction and entering that person's body when he or she starts to drink or use drugs.

This is commonly known as possession. Here are a few examples we have seen of this phenomenon in our work.

Another Round, Please

I once went out to dinner with a friend who was an active alcoholic. I'll call him John. He never drank anything harder than beer, but this particular night he ordered a gin and tonic. As soon as the waiter set down the drink, I saw a male soul enter John's body. I was shocked, but also curious to see what would happen. John ordered three more drinks, and I watched as he became quite intoxicated and obnoxious. When we went back to his house after dinner, he searched for a bottle of hard liquor that he kept for his sister. Then he proceeded to get even more drunk. Just before he passed out, I saw the male spirit leave his body, then turn and smile at me. Immediately, John was out cold.

I called the next day to see how John was. He had no memory of what had happened, from the time we ordered food until he woke up the next morning. I told him he had ordered several gin and tonics. He didn't believe me, because it was so out of character for him.

I never saw that spirit enter John again, and I wondered if the restaurant we had gone to was the spirit's hang-out. It was so creepy to watch him walk right into John's body, and then leave when he had had enough.

I remember one woman who told us that her son could not stay sober. He had gone through treatment and was working with AA. But, from time to time, his personality just changed and he went on a bender. As I investigated, I found that a ghost who had died from alcoholism inhabited the family's home. When I asked the spirit if he took over the young man in order to experience the rush of alcohol, he left the room and didn't want to talk about it. I'm sure that's what was happening. We got rid of the ghost that night, but I never did check back with the woman to see if things had improved for her son.

And remember that bar in Kentucky? Before I was called there to investigate Buck (see chapter 4), I was called there to deal with three spirits who inhabited the bodies of three other men each night and then started fights. They laughed about it and thought it was great fun. When I asked the bar's owner for more details, she said that there was a fight almost every night of the week, usually involving three men who were drinking heavily. The ghosts causing the disturbances were obviously young souls who hadn't learned about karma yet. In fact, all souls who possess the bodies of living people are young souls. They just keep repeating old patterns that they don't want to change.

Move Over, Dear

This next story involves a ghost who wanted to feed her desire for sex. I was in Oregon doing a morning Halloween show for one of the local TV stations there. They took me to a very eerie-looking house and told me only that I was supposed to walk through and

see what I could find. The house was pretty creepy on the inside as well. I saw very little furniture, and the walls were painted purple and black. And there was a man living there. It's hard to explain how I felt, other than to say that I got a very strange vibe.

As I walked through the house, I didn't find much. Until I went up the stairs, that is. That's when I started to feel someone watching me, and I felt a menacing energy as I slowly walked down the hall and around the corner. Out of nowhere, a female spirit came at me very fast and put her hands on my throat.

As you may imagine, I was startled. Who was this woman? And why was she trying to strangle me? I yelled at her to back off, which she did. She told me to stay away from her boyfriend, that he was hers and that they had a sexual relationship. I was dumbfounded. This was the first time I had ever had such an experience. When I asked her what she was talking about, she showed me an image of her going into a young man's body with the intention of havin' sex, and that energy caused them both to experier an orgasm.

I was flabbergasted, to say the least. I didn't know what to tell the producer. I didn't know if I should keep this information to myself, or actually discuss it on television. That was a new dilemma for me. When we got back out to the van, I told the producer what I had seen, and she made the decision not to share the information on the air. Needless to say, I was relieved.

When I told the homeowner what I had heard, he just smiled. He said that every time he brought a woman home for the night, the ghost tried to strangle them as well. I could tell that the ghost had been quite beautiful when she was alive. She had olive skin, wild black hair, and stunning dark eyes. And her energy was very intense. She felt totally in control of this man.

As we went on the air the next morning, the producer told me to "keep it scary," but to give no specific details other than the fact that the spirit had tried to strangle me. My sense about this woman was that she wanted to remain a gorgeous, sexy woman and that she was determined to have these wild love affairs, even though she was deceased.

Another story of possession comes from a suburban home in Minneapolis. The owner of the house in question—we'll call him Tom—seemed timid, but he had a habit of beating up his girlfriend in the middle of the night. Tom was very upset, because he had no memory of his nighttime assaults or of ever hurting his girlfriend. After talking to the couple for a bit, we found it hard to believe that the man would hurt a flea. But they both swore that the events were real. As a consequence, she was afraid to sleep with him.

Michael and I were a bit baffled by this one. During the first hour we spent in the house, we encountered no spirts. Finally, an angry male soul appeared and showed us what he did. He was very angry with a woman who had lived in the house many years before. So every night when Tom fell asleep, the spirit entered his body and began assaulting his girlfriend. When we asked him why, he told us that the girlfriend looked just like the woman who had broken his heart, so he was taking his hurt and anger out on her. It seemed so bizarre.

Our guides said that Tom needed to be very firm and tell this ghost in no uncertain terms to hit the road and not ever come back. At first, Tom didn't think he could do that. We stayed for several hours that night and, eventually, Tom was able to communicate that message to the ghost, whom we then directed into the light.

Turn Me Loose!

A noticeable change in personality is a clear indication that someone is possessed, as we can see in all the stories above. People who are possessed will not look you squarely in the eye and will usually look down during any conversation you may be having with them. Looking directly into their eyes is generally a sure giveaway, because you can see the eyes of the possessing spirit looking back at you.

As a recovering alcoholic, I have had a few experiences with possession—especially back when I was an active drinker myself. It was my psychic teacher, Birdie, who explained that this was what was happening to me when I would wake up in the morning after being totally intoxicated and not remember a thing. A total blackout. My thoughts were not my own. When this happened, I fell prey to very negative, angry feelings and wanted to start drinking right away—something I never did in the morning.

Birdie then gave me some good advice. She told me that, when I was not feeling like myself, I should look in the mirror and see who was looking back at me. At first, I thought she was goofy. I didn't think I would find anybody but myself staring at me in the mirror. But she was right. There were eyes other than my own looking back at me. She told me to hang on to the bathroom sink and demand that the soul leave my body. Then call in Jesus, she said, or some other religious figure and ask that the soul be taken to the other side. This happened to me three times, but the episodes stopped when I finally quit drinking.

It's always been a bit disturbing to me when I encounter souls who do not want to move on to the other side—especially if they want to stay earthbound so they can continue to get high in one way or another. When I was studying with Birdie, she used to say that all the haze in bars is not just cigarette smoke. Half of that haze is the energy of souls, she claimed, just waiting to jump into a body and feel the rush of alcohol or drugs again. Indeed, most alcohol- or drug-addicted souls look for people with a similar serious addiction so they can get their fixes frequently.

A story comes to mind of a friend who was a heavy smoker—two and a half packs a day. When the doctors told him he had lung cancer, he said he would rather die than give up smoking. He refused treatment and continued to smoke heavily. He died shortly thereafter. He was physically addicted, but also mentally and emotionally addicted. He used cigarettes to keep his emotions at bay. I've often wondered how he would get along without smoking on the other side.

People suffering from depression are also susceptible to possession. They often have suicidal thoughts that attract souls who took their own lives. They get stuck in negative patterns that they are not able to change. If you happen to be someone in one of these categories—a depressive personality, an alcoholic, a drug addict, or the victim of any form of addiction—go look at your eyes in a mirror. If the eyes looking back at you are not your own, demand that the soul leave your body *now*. Ask for help from the spirit world to take the spirit over to the other side.

The same can be said of spirit attachments. These are ghosts or earthbound souls who attach themselves to your body, as if they were hitching a ride. The problem is that these spirits can drain your energy, and their thoughts and feelings can influence your own thoughts and feelings. I've heard this phenomenon used to explain all kinds of mental and physical problems over the last few years, but I do not believe it is the only cause of mental or physical maladies, as some psychics and healers claim. If you suspect that there's an entity attached to you or living inside of you, seek out a good shaman who knows how to work with these souls.

A word of warning, however. These services should not cost hundreds or thousands of dollars. There are lots of charlatans out there who claim to be shamans.

Check them out carefully before putting yourself in their hands.

If you are an addict or suffer from depression and your personality changes—if your thoughts sound like someone else's thoughts or are always negative—chances are there is a spirit residing in your body. Don't give it power. Demand that it turn you loose immediately. Don't be wishy-washy about it. You can also call on Jesus, God, the angels, or whatever higher power you believe in to come and take the offending spirit away.

~ Exercise ~

Ask yourself these questions and consider your answers seriously. Do you have an addiction to something that might keep you earthbound? If you do, look at your addiction honestly and ask yourself if it could cause you to remain in this life so you can inhabit another addict's body in order to get drunk or high. Could your attitudes toward sex lead you to live in the body of another in order to continue your sexual experiences? Could your eating habits tempt you to inhabit the body of an overweight person in order to continue eating?

These questions may sound outrageous to those of you who don't have an addiction. But I assure you that these are all real possibilities. Be aware that they exist. Remember, the whole point of this book is to help you move on and learn how to live a happily ever afterlife.

CHAPTER 6

The #1 Reason

Resolve to communicate, evolve, and participate.
Learn, live, love—and go with God.

And now . . . drum roll, please . . . the #1 reason why souls choose not to cross over to the other side.

The #1 reason why souls choose to remain earthbound or roam the astral plane is that they are afraid that God will punish them for something they did in their lifetime. These souls have a strong belief in a punitive God, and were probably raised in strict religious homes. Because the concept of hell—of Satan and fire and brimstone—was strongly impressed upon them, they live in constant fear that they will spend all eternity there. Unsure of whether they are bound for heaven or hell, they simply choose to remain earthbound and refuse to cross over.

We've even had ghosts ask us if we were recruiting souls for hell, and if we worked for Satan. Clearly these souls didn't know what constitutes heaven or hell, or what kind of behavior would land them in one place rather than the other. They probably never asked anyone while they were living, because they were afraid of the answers. So they just stay stuck.

The Power of Beliefs

Have you ever examined your own beliefs about God, Satan, hell, or heaven? As unlikely as it may seem, these beliefs will have a lot to do with your life after death. I've seen souls who believed they were going to hell. When they ended up in heaven, they didn't believe they were really there. It's as if they'd been told that there was only one little amusement park where they could go, and then they found themselves at Disneyland! They weren't sure if it was okay to be there. In fact, they never even knew there was such a place.

Our beliefs come from our families, from a church or organized religion, and from society. They are generational, and we rarely question them. We usually believe what our parents and grandparents believed, and we often don't examine what they told us very carefully. Many of us were probably convinced by one organized religion or another that the world needed to be the way it was and that believing otherwise was sinful. If the church says it is gospel, then it must be so.

But we don't come to Earth looking for rainbows and lollipops. We come here to grow and learn. And a part of this growth and learning is acknowledging how our beliefs may have changed. Ask yourself whether you believe in God, in heaven, in Satan, in hell. And if you do, why do you believe in them? Where did your beliefs come from?

Our Father

Although some don't like to talk about heaven or hell or Satan or God, it's important for all of us to have this discussion. I've had people tell me that they plan to "get straight" with God on their death bed, but that's not really the best time to confront these questions. As you prepare to die, your soul will be going through a process of releasing itself from the body and may not have the opportunity at that point to figure out all these important issues. Your soul will be shifting from heavy, dense earthly energy to a much lighter, more easy-going soul energy. During that process, it probably does not want to be distracted.

I can 100% guarantee, however, that if you develop a good line of communication with God *now*, you'll be able to live much more peacefully in the time you have left in this life. So let's look at your feelings about God. Can you be honest about whatever feelings you have about God? I know that even the word "God" upsets many people because they believe that God is responsible for all the pain and suffering in the world and they don't want anything to do with "Him." But if you are holding on to a lot of fear, or anger, or rage toward God, those feelings can keep you stuck for lifetimes.

Most of us equate God with a male parent. After all, Jesus always instructed us to "go to the Father." Because a lot of people have father issues, however, we project some of those onto God as well. We have to learn to separate our heavenly Father from our earthly father, and put some time and effort into knowing the *real* God.

It's fear of the religious God that makes many afraid of death. We don't feel safe going to God. Religion may have taught us that God is angry or jealous or unforgiving. We may not know where to go when we're in pain. Should we trust or fear God? How do we respond, for instance, to hearing a clergyman claim at a funeral that God wanted a beloved deceased to come home to Him? *What?* How are we supposed to turn to a supreme being for comfort when He's the one who took our loved one away? What a stupid thing to say to someone who is grieving.

My grandmother was a very strict Christian woman. I don't know the particular creed she followed because my dad tried to shelter us from her beliefs. But I know that she had strong feelings about Satan and hell, and when she started to teach me her views, I instinctively tuned her out. I knew that what she was saying wasn't true for me, although I didn't understand why I felt that way. My soul just knew intuitively that her path was not the right path for me.

When I was fourteen, when my parents joined Alcoholics Anonymous, they started talking about God to me and my siblings in a way that was totally different from what my grandmother described. I was fascinated with what they were saying. They talked about a God who was loving and forgiving—just the opposite of what my grandmother had focused on. And that was when I began to feel a desire for a deeper understanding of God and spirituality.

I began reading Emmet Fox's books—especially *The Sermon on the Mount*. What I learned there felt so right to me—intuitively. And nowhere in these beautiful spiritual books did I find any reference to Satan or to hell. I began developing my own beliefs, and, in 2008, wrote a book called *Look for the Good and You'll Find God* that describes my spiritual journey. Now I'm extremely grateful that I learned to seek out my own personal truth at an early age.

If you are someone who has accepted what you've been taught about God, and if these beliefs bring you peace, that's great and I hope you keep growing spiritually. But if you are someone who is not at peace with what you've been taught about life after death, then I urge you to take a deeper look. We know through our intuition—that gut feeling—when something is off. If you feel unsettled when thinking about life after death, take a closer look at your other beliefs. If you have friends who seem very much at peace with their beliefs, ask them about them. Just make sure that you stay detached enough to hear a response from your own inner voice. Remember that our souls are all at different levels of development (see chapter 4). So what fits for them may not fit for you. You have your own unique life path to follow.

That Pesky Ego

Many spiritual teachers say that we must tame our egos in order to grow spiritually. For the longest time, I didn't understand that, but it's become more clear to me as time passes just how destructive or enabling our egos can be. Our egos can actually interfere with us having a loving relationship with God, because they want to believe that they are in control.

I teach a weekly class on the life of Jesus. We've been meeting for five years, studying books by different authors. We let our intuition guide us as we choose these books and, at the end of each class, I lead a guided meditation based on the lesson of the day. The process has always been very rewarding and our experiences together are always so special.

One of the books we explored in this class is *The Jesus Trilogy*, by Gina Lake. In it, Lake makes this comment about the ego:

Ego is not meant to be the master creator of your life. It is the aspect of the human being that creates conflict, complications, confusion, unpleasant emotions, and bad karma. How can something like that create a beautiful and fulfilling life? And yet, that is what is at the helm of most people's lives (p. 198).

She goes on to talk about the ego as a false self—the part of ourselves we show to the world. But the ego, she warns us, just gets in our way and hurts us most of our lives.

Lake's book made me more aware of my own ego, my outer shell—the "me" I present to the world versus the real me, my soul. My ego gets caught up in meeting expectations of what others expect of me and I can lose myself. Here's a personal story to show you what I mean. I think you'll be able to relate to it in one way or another.

Beautiful People

I grew up with a beautiful, slender mother who had done a bit of modeling, and a father with a big ego. He loved taking my mother out in public because people always commented on how beautiful she was, and that fed his ego. When I was fourteen, my father sent me to modeling school, hoping I would turn out like my mother. But then I started putting on weight and he didn't like that. Whenever I lost weight, my dad was very approving of me. But when I gained weight back, he gave me disgusted looks. I hated that pressure, so I was constantly watching what I ate, getting on the scale, and then rebelling and eating anything and everything I wanted to. This became a vicious cycle in my life—a destructive pattern that kept my soul from growing.

When I started dating men, they were all like my dad, with the exception of one or two. They were very disappointed if my body wasn't that of a gorgeous model. And when *they* weren't putting pressure on me, I was putting pressure on myself. Then I realized that I had probably been like these men in a previous life and that I came here to this lifetime to experience the whole thing from a woman's perspective. I think that, in a previous lifetime, I had treated women like arm candy, and judged them based on their appearance rather than on any of their other qualities.

This emphasis on women's physical appearance is a particularly destructive, ego-driven behavior for those who are overweight in today's society. I'm working on breaking this egoic pattern—deciding how I want to look and feel, getting to that goal, and learning to be happy with myself instead of always being self-critical. As they say, life here is not for sissies.

Ego-ick Patterns

Some believe that souls don't have egos, but I don't believe that's correct. I've met many souls on the other side who have egos. Take, for example, a young boy who was featured in a recent television show called *The Ghost Inside My Child*. The boy had night terrors in which he relived how he had died in his most recent past life. At a very young age, he began begging his parents to take him to Hollywood, although no one could figure out why, because they had never even talked about Hollywood. Finally, after a number of "coincidences," the boy and his mother went to Hollywood, and to a particular museum there where his ego was, at last, satisfied. The boy's ego had apparently communicated that he had been cheated by an early death in his previous life. After the trip to Hollywood, the boy's night terrors stopped and he was finally able to live a normal life.

The patterns we are forced into by our egos can be destructive both to ourselves and to the people in our lives. And these patterns can be carried across the threshold of death and back again to shape multiple lifetimes.

To break out of these patterns, you must first become aware of them. Ask yourself why you do the things you do—why you say the things you say. Try to identify the patterns that your false self imposes on you. Do you base your own self-worth on your spouse's appearance? Do you measure how good a parent you are by your children's successes or failures? Do you define yourself by your position at the place where you work? Do you constantly brag about your accomplishments? Or do you walk around with no confidence trying to convince others that you're amazing? Is your ego hiding the real you?

We have to keep an eye out for our egos because they cause us to make bad choices in hopes that people will like us. Do you try to keep up with the Joneses? Do you rely on the opinion of others to make you feel successful or desireable? Do you say "yes" to things when you want to say "no"? Do you let others dictate how you respond to situations and challenges? These are all destructive patterns that are driven by our egos' desire to control us and define who we are.

Remember those poor ghosts left earthbound or stranded on the astral plane? If they were being their true authentic selves, living according to guidance from within rather than according to the demands of their egos, I don't think they'd be stuck here. It boggles my mind how we allow our egos to keep us stuck in destructive patterns lifetime after lifetime.

I can't stress this enough. There are too many ghosts hanging out on the earthly and astral planes, scared to death (pun intended) to move on to the other side because of what they've been taught—either by their egos or by beliefs that have been imposed on them by family, by friends, by religion, or by society at large. I want you to be happy now *and* in the afterlife. If you have strong beliefs in Satan and hell, examine why and ask yourself if they feel true to you. When it's your time to leave your physical body and move over to the other side, I want you to skip on over that threshold and begin a happily ever afterlife. This is the time for you to rest, relax, and heal—not burn in hell for eternity or roam the earthly plane looking for satisfaction.

Remember this: Negative beliefs that are deeply held become real. But positive beliefs that are held deeply also become real. *Your choice.*

~ *Exercise* ~

If you don't think you're worthy of a wonderful after-life, ask yourself why. I have a hunch that one or two reasons will come to mind right away. List all the reasons you can think of and write them down. No one need see your list if you don't want them to. Then ask yourself where these beliefs came from and why you keep holding on to them. Did they come from family? Society? Religion?

If you answer that your beliefs came from the Bible, consider that they are grounded in a consciousness that is 2000 years old. I've got nothing against the Bible. It's a wonderful book that is loaded with knowledge, wisdom, and reassurance. But it's also loaded with outdated information. God gave you the gift of discernment and, if you want to live according to the Bible, you have to use that gift and pay close attention to what your intuition tells you. This is particularly true if the Bible is the source of your beliefs about death and the afterlife. If this is the case, write out all the biblical teachings that are causing you fear, then run them by your inner voice.

CHAPTER 7

Random Reasons

When you give the truth you know,
Observe how well the garden grows.

So far, we've looked at six main reasons why souls choose to remain on the earthly plane after death. They don't know (or don't want to admit) that they're dead. They don't like change. They want to avoid someone on the other side. They don't believe there's anything after death. They stay here to feed addictions. Or they are afraid of God or Satan or hell.

But there are many other less obvious reasons as well. One that comes to mind right away is that some souls think that life in heaven consists of praying all day or constantly singing praises to God. Other souls think they can't fall in love or have relationships on the other side, so they stay here trying to establish relationships with living beings. We saw in chapter 2 that ghosts don't like change, and that they tend to stay put once they find a situation where they are comfortable. Some literally stay in one place—one location—even if that's a particular spot in a huge home or building. One ghost I met lived in his car because he loved it so much.

We've even seen ghosts who have fallen in love with someone whose house is on the market and have done whatever they could to keep the house from selling—making noises, playing with electronics, or standing by the front door to scare away potential buyers. That's when we get calls from realtors saying the house is perfect, and they can't understand why clients get up to the front door and then turn around and leave. Whenever we counsel ghosts in situations like these, we reassure them that souls can and do have relationships in heaven. We don't stop loving just because our physical bodies have died.

The souls of teenagers often fear that heaven is going to be boring. They don't want to become angels who fly around on wings. They'd rather stay here, where they can go to parties. I once ghostbusted a high school that was being haunted by thirty-four teenaged souls and one deceased teacher. All of them believed that, once they died, they would no longer have fun, so they just stayed put. And we once cleared a ghost who sang opera every night and pulled a teenage daughter's hair when she disrespected her mother. She said that she was the "nanny" of the neighborhood and that she kept the teenagers in line.

Other souls stay put because of a desire for justice. I once saw deceased actor/comedian John Belushi screaming that he had been ripped off. He was very angry that he was dead and claimed that the woman with whom he had been having a relationship had caused his overdose. It was really sad to see how tormented he was, floating around the astral plane looking for justice.

Equally strong is the desire to protect. We once did a ghostbusting in a house that was haunted by a woman's murdered brother. He was worried that the man who had murdered him would come back and murder her as well. When we checked it out psychically to see if that might happen, we found that the murderer was long gone. But this soul just couldn't let it go. He felt strongly that he needed to stay there and protect his sister.

We've also known of cases where the original builders of homes stick around to make sure no one makes any changes to their houses. People in the home are unaware of anything suspicious until they start making plans to change the home in some way—perhaps add another room or make major changes to some part of the house. We always let these deceased builders know that they can build new homes on the other side.

And then there was the ghost who kept scaring everyone working at a warehouse. The warehouse had been built on land that this ghost had owned when he was alive. He hated the ugly tin building and wanted it torn down so the area could return to its natural state. He literally slapped me on the back of my neck and told me to get out of there. It takes a lot of anger for a ghost to harm someone physically, and

I was quite surprised. But it was my fear that gave him the energy to do that. We could not convince this ghost to move on, so we left.

Helping Hands

We are often asked why deceased loved ones or spirit guides don't come and help the souls who are stuck here. The answer is that they do. But it gets complicated when the deceased don't want to go. Nobody can force a soul against its will—although there are exceptions. When a person dies of an overdose, for example, that person's soul is also affected by the drugs. If the soul is unconscious, we've seen angels come and retrieve it and take it home. When the soul becomes conscious again, caregivers on the other side help it understand what has happened.

Some souls think they are in a kind of strange dream when they leave the body. It can take a few days for them to realize what has occurred. I remember when a well-known actor—a client of my brother—accidentally died from asphyxiation. I wanted to check to make sure that he had made it over into the light. What I discovered was that he thought he was having a bad dream. His soul remained in his closet for three days before finally believing what his spirit guides were telling him—that he had actually died. His ego simply would not accept his death. It felt that the actor should live on forever because he was such a famous person.

In the majority of deaths, we see our deceased loved ones as soon as our own souls pass out of our bodies. In fact, most souls are accompanied to the other side by someone who was dear to them. A great example of this is my own experience with the Columbine shootings, which killed so many children. When I saw the report on the news, I checked in on the children immediately. I was very happy to see that most of them had been met by deceased grandparents who were waiting for them right there at the school when their souls came out of their bodies. They immediately reassured the children and took them over to the other side.

There was one child, however, who went over alone. She was an old soul who knew right where to go. The soul of another child went to his physical home to be close to his mother. The two of them lived alone and he was very worried about her. When his grandparents tried to talk him into moving to the other side, he refused to go. He remained with his mother until a year later, when she committed suicide. Then the two of them crossed over together.

Long after I began pondering these questions, I was introduced to the Squadron, a group of former ghosts who now reside on the other side. They explained that they visit many haunted places, doing their best to convince the ghosts they find to go home with them. They talk to them about their beliefs and fears, reassuring them that heaven is very different from what they may think. The Squadron's leader told me that we could call on them whenever we got calls for help from people we couldn't visit personally. We just need to tell them where the problem is, and they will help. I have called on them several times for help with people from out of town who requested our services. I have heard many glowing reports from these people after their problems were resolved. Let's hear it for the helping hands of the Squadron!

Young Souls

Death is different for everyone, and we all have reasons why we either go right home to heaven or stay earthbound. But I've always been troubled about the spirits of children—and especially newborns. Why don't angels or deceased loved ones come and get them? And why do these souls still identify themselves as children? When a baby is born, an adult soul enters its body. So if the child dies at an early age, why doesn't that soul revert back to being an adult? My guess is that they themselves are young souls who don't want to revert. Or perhaps they are very young souls who don't even know that they can.

Here's an example. Back in the 1990s, I appeared on a segment of a popular TV show called *The Other*

Side. In that show, I met with homeowners who could hear a ball bouncing in their upstairs game room. There *was* a ball in the room, but no one ever went up there. When I entered the room, I immediately saw the spirits of six children. When I asked the soul of one little girl what they were doing there, she answered that they were playing with the ball. The producer wanted me to get the children to move the ball, but moving physical objects on demand can be quite challenging for young spirits. It takes a lot of energy for them to do that, and they generally need to get that energy from someone or something in the room—people, pets, or plants.

When I asked the children why they were in that particular home, they said it was because of the ball and that they didn't know where else to go. When I asked them how they had died, one of them said they had died in a fire, but didn't elaborate. After the taping of the show was over, the homeowner told us that there had been an orphanage down the block a very long time ago. That building had burned down, and several children had perished in the fire.

So again, my question is, why hasn't anyone come from the other side to bring these children over? And why are the children's souls choosing to be children instead of the adult souls that they are? I have come to believe that the souls of children continue to define themselves as children rather than as adults because they are in a learning process. As young souls, they have little awareness of the bigger picture, so this is how they see themselves. And there's no pressure for any soul to see itself as an adult. Once these young souls get over to the other side, however, they begin to see things differently. And there are many helping hands there to assist them as they make the transition from thinking of themselves as solitary, earthbound children, to seeing themselves with greater clarity as adult souls living in heaven.

As far as why beings from the other side don't come and take the souls of children home—they do. As we have seen, angels and groups like the Squadron, who help earthbound adult ghosts cross over, do the same for earthbound children.

We were once called to a home where an eight-year-old daughter refused to sleep in her room. The parents had done everything they could to make her bed and bedroom appealing to her, but nothing worked. With a sense of desperation, they called us. We walked through the house and found nothing resembling a spirit—until we got to the daughter's bedroom. There were at least eight spirits of children piled on top of her bed. They had been trapped inside some kind of time warp long ago, and had all remained earthbound together.

The spirits of these children seemed mentally off to us. They didn't respond to us when we asked them the usual questions—like what their names were and why they were there. One of our guides told us that there had once been an insane asylum on this property, and that many of the people who had died there remained earthbound. We asked the angels to come and take the children's souls to the other side, and that's exactly what they did. Every one of them followed the angels home. The homeowner later told us that, after some research, he learned that there had, indeed, once been an asylum on his property.

Energy Vampires

Medical science tells us that a soul weighs approximately twenty-one grams. They know this from having weighed bodies both immediately before and immediately after death. So how can a spirit that weighs only twenty-one grams pick up material objects and make them move? They need energy from someone or from somewhere. Remember Buck? And we've definitely seen a connection between very active ghosts and others living in a home who suffer from maladies like chronic fatigue.

Many years ago, I had the pleasure of meeting Farrah Fawcett when a production company was making a six-episode series called *Chasing Farrah*. The actress wanted me to see if she had a ghost in her home. Her energy was extremely low, and I wondered if there was a spirit sucking her energy from her. When I entered the house, I was drawn to an area in the corner of her bedroom. I didn't see a spirit there, but my guides told me to tell her to put a large plant in that area so that whatever was feeding off her energy could feed off the plant instead.

Looking back, I wish I had had more time to channel healing to the actress. She was extremely fragile and I wanted to spend at least an hour healing her, but production schedules and constraints wouldn't allow it. I was able to channel some healing to her when we were sitting in the living room, however. Unbeknownst to me, the crew was recording the healing session and decided to use that scene in the show. Unfortunately, we were all caught up in the moment, and I left when the filming was over. Days later, Farrah found out that she had cancer. Although she was so tiny and fragile, she fought the cancer fiercely. Unfortunately for all of us who loved her, she passed away not long after.

~ Exercise ~

Did you see yourself in any of these stories? Did you find in them any reasons why you might possibly choose to remain earthbound? If none of these stories resonates with you, can you think of any other random reason why you might choose to stay here? As you answer these questions, think about whether there is anything in your life or in your beliefs that might cause you to avoid crossing over.

When the owner of a coffee shop once recognized me as the author of *Relax, It's Only a Ghost*, he proudly announced to everyone in the shop that he was definitely going to be a ghost when he died, because he thought it sounded like a lot of fun to haunt people and scare them. Is that something that appeals to you?

CHAPTER 8

Safe Passage

Life and death are movements within a symphony.
Some things change, some stay the same, almost as in
a dream.
Eyes open or eyes closed, you'll see what you will see.
The doorway is open to a world of possibilities.

So we've talked about the afterlife. Now let's talk about death.

Many people have a tremendous fear of death. Think of your body as the vehicle of your soul. It is through your body that you've gotten around on this earthly plane. But what if one day, when this vehicle was driving along, its transmission failed and it just broke down? Or what if your vehicle broke down more slowly—as the parts failed one by one—until, finally, it just ground to a halt? When our cars die, of course, we can buy a new one. But when the vehicle of your body dies, that's it. And the fact is that both our cars and our bodies can benefit from better fuel and regular maintenance.

You can tell if a soul is still attached to a body by the movements and sounds coming from the body—by how the vehicle handles, so to speak. When a soul has detached itself, the body is very quiet and its breathing is quite shallow. Very sensitive people in the presence of someone dying may even be able feel when the soul is no longer present or when it departs.

Fear of Dying

I believe that, when your current life is complete, the actual act of dying is one of the easiest things you'll ever do. If you are an old soul—Level 3 or especially Level 4—your soul may even leave days before your actual death takes place. Old souls remember that they have been through the dying process hundreds of times, and that it's not necessary to stick around until the last breath is drawn.

But younger souls may not remember what dying feels like, so they may fight it. People have asked me why a loved one was taking so long to die, or why God was making their loved one suffer through a long, painful death. I remember one young man who learned in his late twenties or early thirties that he had brain cancer. He tried to postpone his death for as long as possible, fighting very hard to prolong his life and putting his body through hell. His family also went through a lot of suffering during his dying process. He had a beautiful young wife and a lifetime of plans, and he didn't want to let go. So you can see why this was such a struggle for him.

But I can tell you this with assurance. It is not God who makes us suffer as we die. Rather it's our own fears that cause us to hang on to life and fight death. And these fears are usually found in people who have strong, negative beliefs about death and the afterlife.

Sometimes, when it seems as if someone is taking a long time to die, it can be because the soul is hoping that a prolonged dying process will help family members come together and heal. I've seen many families whose members were estranged make amends and heal emotional wounds when they came together to say a final goodbye to a loved one. Usually, the person's death occurs right after the reconciliation. A lot of unfinished family business can be resolved during the death of a loved one.

But dying is about what's next, not about what's past. It's about surrendering to the next great adventure. That's why we should all live as best we can while we're here. And when it's time to move into that great beautiful light, it's better to go with no regrets, anticipating what is yet to come in the next episode of our existence.

So what are you afraid of? If you die in an accident or a plane crash, your soul will leave your body before impact, so you won't feel any pain. And even if you live through something like that, your soul steps out while the accident is happening. That's why people never remember the actual moment of impact when they are involved in accidents.

Dying need not entail suffering. We only suffer when our conscious minds fight the process. If you can't overcome your fear of a painful death, just tell your soul that you want your passage to be easy and painless. Let your soul take it from there.

Seeing Is Believing—And Vice Versa

Our beliefs control the majority of our earthly lives and how we perceive the afterlife. Those who believe in an afterlife have preconceptions about what that experience will be like. But those ideas can be wrong. My out-of-body journeys to the other side have always been positive. I don't know exactly what I believed about heaven before I had these experiences, but I know that what I saw on these journeys was always happy, loving, and positive.

On one journey, I saw the twelve-year-old son of my best friend playing basketball. He said a quick hello as he tossed the ball through the hoop. I remember being startled that he was playing a game known for having very tall players. During life, my friend's son had been small in stature, compared to his very tall sister, who had inherited her height from their 6'8" father. The son was more like his 5'5" mother. It struck me as remarkable and fortunate that he could now be the height he had wanted to be when he was alive.

This is why I continually ask about your beliefs, because heaven is no more or less than what you believe is possible. Your life in heaven is going to be loving and positive *if you let it be.* How would you feel if you could fish, or play golf, or play baseball all the time? What if you could work at something you love? Or invent new things to make life on Earth easier? Or take better care of yourself? Imagine yourself in a loving relationship, or going to school, or joining a church, or living in communities similar to the ones you've lived in on Earth. No more physical problems, no allergies, no stress. Whatever your beliefs are in this life, they will shape your heaven. The possibilities are endless.

And the natural world is even more gorgeous on the other side. The colors are ten times brighter than they are here. And animals are everywhere. Music of all kinds fills the air if you want it to, and musicians are always busy writing new songs. Doctors are working on cures for physical ailments. Angels are out and about, and everyone has a home. We may feel grief when a loved one leaves for a life on Earth, but it's a different kind of grief, because we know that we can check in on them throughout their lifetime.

In short, life in heaven is amazing—just as amazing as you care to make it. Yes, you can see your deceased loved ones, and God, and anyone else who is significant to you. And there are many unique communities. You can live in a community that reflects your expectations, since it's actually your beliefs that create that community.

I even saw a community once that was supposed to represent hell. When my angel guide pointed it out to me during one of my journeys, I laughed at first. It had such a different feel to it. Imagine a field of white blossoms with a dark, lifeless patch of barren ground off to one side, making a startling contrast to all the flowers. When I asked what it was, my guide said that, since so many souls believed they were going to hell, their thoughts actually created that experience. The community I saw was dark inside, and appeared to be permeated by fire. In fact, it looked exactly the way I would expect a stage set of hell to look. I saw souls walking around in there with no energy, no life—souls who believed that this was where they were meant to be.

At some point, however, these souls will start asking questions. And someone on the other side will then explain that it was their beliefs that sent them to this hell, and that the afterlife is not about punishment and eternal suffering. If they are willing to change their beliefs, these souls can escape their self-created hell and begin to grow beyond that limited experience. They may even look for loved ones or seek counsel from the wise Elders about what's next for them (see chapter 9). Eventually they learn, as we all do, that it wasn't God who created this hellish place. It was their own beliefs. And it can take lifetimes to let them go.

~ *Exercise* ~

So, for the very last time, I ask you to consider what your beliefs are about the afterlife. Remember, my friend—you are a child of God. That means you are worthy of so much goodness and love. Please don't let negative beliefs about yourself, about heaven, or about God keep you stuck on the earthly plane. You deserve a wonderful, happily ever afterlife, instead of hanging around in purgatory or in someone's attic. It doesn't matter what the people around you believe. This is about *you* moving on to what's next.

Heaven will be everything you want it to be, if you open your beliefs to all the goodness available to you. Life on Earth is hard and crazy, fulfilling and disappointing, happy and sad. Let yourself know and believe that you get to have a happily ever afterlife— and it shall be done.

CHAPTER 9

Lessons Learned

For years, I have said that my gift of prophecy is a curse because I see so many things I don't want to see. I feel people's pain, and I see the unhappiness in their lives. I see into the private lives of others and may see unpleasant things in their future. This gives me a heavy responsibility to act ethically, and to give painful information with love and compassion. I have had to learn how to separate my feelings, my beliefs, and my judgments, and only bring through information that will be helpful to those who ask for my guidance. As hard as that has been, I'm also very grateful to have these gifts. I get to see such beautiful episodes in other people's lives, and I've been fortunate to learn everything I'm sharing with you by developing these abilities.

It's so important for all of us to keep a balance in our lives—to keep our feet firmly planted on the ground. We don't want to become disoriented when living between the dimensions of the earthly plane and the other side. I say this because I want to take this book beyond just ghost stories and reasons why souls choose to remain earthbound. I want you to learn from it and to use these lessons to make your life—and your death—easier. Over the years, I have begun to understand more about the greater reality of our purpose here on Earth, and I want to share these insights with you.

We all have many questions about life. Why are we here? Why do we have to go through so many challenges? Why does God allow all this misery? Why doesn't God save us from pain? Why do we have to die, and why do our loved ones have to die? Why, why, why? I can't give you all the answers—especially to questions about how life began, or who created our world, or who created God. But I can share with you my own view about the path our souls are on.

Body and Soul

Do you ever think much about your soul? When you were young, you may have said the same bedtime prayer that I did:

> *Now I lay me down to sleep.*
> *I pray the Lord my soul to keep.*
> *If I should die before I wake,*
> *I pray the Lord my soul to take.*

That innocent reference to the soul was about all I knew about souls until I started doing my work as a psychic and a healer.

Nor did I know much about ghosts. I thought they were just blobby masses of energy that scared people. It wasn't until I started putting two and two together that I realized that ghosts were actually the souls of those who had lived on Earth. After that "aha" moment, I became intrigued with souls. Does everyone have one? Does the soul look like its body? Does the soul think or have feelings? What part does it play in our physical world? And why do we come here in the first place? I started asking these and so many other questions. But I didn't start getting answers until I started healing people.

One experience in particular started me on my path. It involved a fourteen-year-old boy who was in a coma. He had landed on his head after falling eighteen feet, and had been airlifted from Nebraska to Minneapolis for treatment at the University of Minnesota. His step-mom contacted me, asking me to meet them at the hospital to do a healing on him. I walked into the boy's room just as the nurse was telling the family that it was doubtful he would ever come out of the coma. And if he did, she said, it was unlikely that he would be able to walk or feed himself. The nurse commented that they could save themselves a lot of money by putting him in a nursing home, rather than keeping him in the hospital.

The medical prognosis was horrible. It filled everyone in the room with fear. I needed a break from the tension, so I excused myself to go for a walk. I silently asked God if he had heard what the nurse had said. A voice replied: "Don't listen to the fears of the world. Get to work." And that's exactly what I did. I channeled healing to that boy every day for six weeks. In the end, he walked out of the hospital on his own, chatting away with his family.

But the really fascinating part of this story took place on the second day that I visited the boy. And what happened that day helped me understand much more about souls.

As I stood over the boy with one hand on his head and the other on his heart, I suddenly heard a male voice that seemed to come from behind me saying that he wanted me to focus my healing on the part of the brain that affects speech. I could feel the presence of someone, but there was no one else in the room besides the boy and myself. I slowly turned and saw a ghostly figure leaning against the wall—a young man in blue jeans and a T-shirt. When I asked the figure who he was, he said he was the soul of the boy in the coma.

Needless to say, I was astonished. The figure was so nonchalant about it, as if I should have known this. When I asked him how he could be outside the boy's body, he said that souls come and go all the time and that the body doesn't feel pain when the soul is not present. So he was choosing to stay outside for now. There was no risk of his getting lost, because he was attached to the boy's body by a silver cord.

Every time I went to the hospital after that, this figure appeared and told me what the boy's body needed that day. Sometimes his knees hurt; sometimes he had an ache in his head or neck. We communicated like this until the boy came out of the coma. At that point, I knew intuitively that he didn't need further healings. He worked with a physical therapist to learn how to walk again, and left the hospital under his own power.

After that experience, whenever I did a healing, I silently asked to communicate with the patient's soul because I now realized that the soul was in charge of how things would go. Our bodies are just a vehicle—a way to get around. Imagine watching an astronaut move about in space. It may appear that the space suit is in charge, but it's the body inside that is really running the show. The same relationship exists between bodies and souls.

My experience with this young boy taught me the answers to some of the questions we all ask about life.

- Does everyone have a soul? Yes, every living being, including every animal, has a soul.
- Does that soul look like its body? All the souls I have seen look like their bodies, except that they look younger.
- Does the soul think or have feelings? Yes, definitely.
- Why do we come here, and what part do our souls play in the physical world?

The rest of this chapter will address this question.

But first, we need to talk about God.

It's All About Energy

The Bible tells us that we are made in the image and likeness of God, so I always thought that meant that God was white—after all, I'm white, so God must be white. Everyone called God "him," so I assumed he must look like a white male—kind of like Santa Claus without the jolly personality. Religion teaches us that God is angry, jealous, and punishing, so I always imagined him with a scowl on his face. It was not a comforting image I had built. But since then, I've learned to see God in a completely different light.

I know now that God is *energy*. That may be hard to wrap your head around, but try. Try to visualize energy—energy that may appear in human form, but also in many other forms. I once asked God in meditation what he looked like and he said it depends on who's asking. (To keep things simple, I will continue to use the masculine pronoun here.) He said that, if a tree asked him that question, he would appear as a tree, because that's all the tree understands. If a lion asked, he would appear as a lion. When people ask, he appears as a human. What's important, he said, is that he is a very loving, creative, compassionate energy that is not limited to just one form. Moreover, that energy is both male and female—in perfect balance.

As a creative energy, God can't help but create. Just look around at the beauty of our natural world—the sky, the land, the flowers, the rivers, the oceans, the mountains, the seasons. God's energy created it all. And it also created our souls, which are themselves energy. Our personalities consist of energy projected by our souls. Our subconscious minds are projections of the energy of our souls. In fact, at the most essential level, we are *simply energy*.

In my meditations, I've seen that when we were first created, we were all stars that existed to light up the night sky. At some point in our existence, however, we felt an inner nudging to grow into more. And when we yearned to become more, our cycles of reincarnation began. Perhaps you began your existence as an animal. Have you ever felt a strong affinity to a particular pre-historic animal? Remember, your soul has actually been around for a very long time.

I believe that God took a part of himself—his energy—and planted it inside of each of us so that we could always be guided by spirit. This essence is a beautiful light that shines inside us that is constantly available to us when we need help. Our souls rely on this internal spark throughout our many lifetimes. But as we became more educated and more intellectual, we began to rely more on our minds and stopped listening to this inner voice. And when we gave over so much power to our minds—to our egos—we no longer felt our own divine connection to God's energy—to our Creator. And that's when we began to feel as if we were all alone.

Soul School

The purpose of having several lifetimes is to develop our souls to their highest potential. There's no way we can do that in one lifetime. Imagine humans evolving out of the primordial slime to become humanity as we know it today in the span of just one lifetime. In fact, it took many lifetimes of experiences for you to become the person you are now. And every experience you went through was an important opportunity for you to grow. Our lives in this world are based on what we need and want to learn, and what patterns we create over time that need to be healed in order for us to move forward.

I knew one woman who had more physical problems than anyone I had ever met and she wanted to know why. When I asked my guides, they told me that her soul's goal was to be a doctor in her next life, and she wanted to gather as much information as she could regarding sickness in this life. She told me afterward that she had always had a feeling that she was going to be a doctor, but that she couldn't see any way for that to happen in this lifetime because of financial limitations.

Between our lifetimes, a group of souls known as the Elders help us plan for our next incarnation here on Earth, or even on other planets. Your soul feels an inner desire to grow more, so you go to the Elders and ask for help in creating your next life. A record of all of our life experiences is stored in what's known as the Akashic record. The Elders go through your record to see how much you have grown, how far you have come, and what is left for you to experience. Depending upon the level your soul has reached, you may have a say in what you want to experience.

The Elders' plan for you includes your appearance and your culture, as well as the date, time, and place of your birth. That is why astrology can help you see connections between your life and the heavens. Each planet represents something very unique, and the placement of the houses in your chart can tell you a great deal about your life plan. Numerology is another tool you can use to understand yourself and what you are here to experience.

Planning a lifetime is no easy task. It takes a lot of time. Our families are chosen based on what we need to accomplish in our new life. Believe it or not, our families are the best reflections of what we came here to experience. Some of you probably can't imagine how your dysfunctional family could have been cho-sen for your benefit, but they were. We learn much from the experiences we have with our families. If one member of a family is going through something mean-ingful, the rest of the family goes through it as well, learning as they go.

Let's say you grew up with an abusive, alcoholic parent—perhaps an alcoholic father and a codepen-dent mother, or vice versa. What patterns might you be carrying from a previous life that caused you to be born into that family? Your soul may be suffer-ing from alcoholism or some other mood-altering addiction from a past life, and it is your goal to finally recover from that in this new life. Your addic-tions may have led you to establish a pattern of code-pendency and a feeling that the only way to be loved was to make everyone else in your life happy. So you put others before yourself, ignoring your own need to learn to love yourself. A pattern like this can be particularly destructive because, when you become dependent on others for any good feelings you have about yourself, you end up being miserable and resentful of people for always taking from you and never giving anything back.

My guides have told me that this is a common issue on Earth, and that part of a person's life plan may be to heal this pattern. These individuals' life purpose may be two-fold: to heal from their own addictions and learn how to take care of themselves, and to let others learn how to take care of themselves. These two patterns can be very difficult to heal, and it can take lifetimes to break them.

Some say that we develop our patterns by the age of seven. In the life pattern described above, you may have found yourself surrounded by the very patterns you are here to heal. Each member of your family is part of your plan, and you can learn valuable lessons from them. The same is true whether you grew up in a single-parent family, or even in an orphanage. Without a "typical" family, you may gravitate to people who can fill in the gaps in your life and create a different kind of family.

Indeed, the first seven years of our lifetime provide good clues about what patterns we are here to heal.

People often ask me why someone would choose to grow up in poverty or starving in a third-world country. Why would any soul choose that for a life lesson? The answer is simple. To grow from the experience. If you were quite wealthy in a past life and looked down on the poor, for instance, you may be here now to walk in their shoes and learn compassion for them. Or you may be here to help the poor, or create new ways to provide them with food, or water, or clothing, or shelter.

The lives we live aren't random. There is purpose in everything, and every experience in life is an opportunity. Learning compassion may be an important reason why you came to Earth. Stop for a few minutes and think about living in poverty. What do you think you could learn from that lifestyle?

The Money Trap

Money is a powerful motivator in life, and one that can teach us important life lessons. Most people believe that money translates into power and security.

Have you ever wondered why some people do very little work and make a ton of money, while others seem to work long hours and earn just enough to get by? And what about those millions of others who spend money trying to win the lottery when they know the odds are overwhelmingly against them? But we can learn a lot about our life patterns by examining the patterns we establish around money.

My dad grew up relatively poor, determined to become a wealthy man. He worked really hard and, when I was fourteen, we moved to a wealthy suburb in Minnesota. The improvement in our circumstances didn't happen all at once, however. As a kid, I remember eating a lot of hot dogs, mac and cheese, TV dinners, and casseroles. When we started having an occasional steak for dinner, my dad told us that we were eating like rich people.

We lived in a small, three-bedroom home. And then one day, my dad bought himself an expensive car and my parents told us we were moving to a new house in a new neighborhood. We were excited that we'd each have a bedroom of our own! We suddenly had new clothes, fancy cars, family trips, and a brand new sixteen-room home.

Dad said we were rich, but I wasn't even sure what that meant. I liked my old way of life. Things seemed easier. Now, everything was new and the people in our neighborhood were different from my former friends. And no matter what we had, it never seemed to be enough for my dad. He worked harder, bought expensive boats, and our lifestyle changed again.

Dad got very involved in philanthropy and he seemed happy. But throughout this whole money journey, my inner voice told me to observe the experience but not to get locked into it. It was okay to have the experience of what it was like to have money, but my intuition warned me to wear it like a loose garment. Don't hold on too tightly to the idea of being rich, my inner voice told me. For me, the experience always had a temporary feeling to it.

As my dad got older, he started spending more than he was making and ended up in bankruptcy.

He became discouraged and depressed. Personally, I think he never felt worthy of being rich. He had grown up with a different mentality and wasn't able to adjust and learn how to be comfortable as a wealthy man. He ended up losing everything. When he died, he was living on welfare. He felt like a total failure.

My hope for my father is that, during his life review on the other side, he came to see his experiences from a higher perspective, understanding what he had learned and seeing the impact that money can have on a person. For some in my family, my father's pattern was repeated—at least two others went from being rich to being broke pretty quickly. Although it's easy to say that money should not define our self-worth, that's often how it is in this world. We all have a lot to learn about money in this life. One of the valuable lessons I've learned is that money is not security. It only seems that way. Real security comes from within, and that can take lifetimes to learn.

Stop for a moment and ask yourself whether there are lessons about money that you need to learn in this lifetime.

Not in Kansas Anymore

In fact, there are many lessons we may be here to learn in this school called life. These lessons relate to many different facets of our existence here on Earth, including:

- Money and relationships (family, friends, acquaintances, enemies, pets)
- Heritage, parenting, and work (ethics, career and job choices)
- Race, religion, and faith
- Fame and security
- Politics and societal beliefs
- Birth and loss
- Stress and addictions
- Nutrition, physical health, and handicaps (physical, mental, and emotional challenges)

Our souls learn these lessons at each soul level. When we are younger souls, we interpret everything as if we were victims of circumstance. As our souls grow in consciousness, however, we come to understand that the experiences we are having are teaching us.

There are also outside forces that help to teach us life lessons. The planets each have a purpose, and definitely have an impact on our lives. As I write this book in June, 2021, the planet Neptune is retrograde, and this is how one astrologer explained the significance of this to me:

In the Wizard of Oz, Dorothy is thrown into a tornado that takes her to the land of Oz. She watches as strange things fly by her—a barn, a bicycle, a chicken, a cow. She could try to grab on to these things to get a grip on something solid and familiar, but it would quickly get ripped out of her hands. She is in a tornado! The only thing she can do is surrender to the winds and have faith that she'll end up in the right place.

Dorothy lands in a fantastical world where the rules she has known all her life no longer apply, and the rules that do apply don't make sense. No matter what she does, she can't seem to find her way—at least not on her own. She falters and is awash in confusion. But along the way, she finds guides, she overcomes challenges, and she vanquishes her demons. That journey eventually leads her to her ultimate realization. She discovers that she has had her own internal compass all along, and it points her to the only real home any of us can ever have—herself.

That is the point of Neptune. Have faith in the journey, no matter how strange it seems. When all is said and done, you'll have a core, a little kernel of self that remains untouched by the fog. And that piece is the home we can return to again and again. We may get lost and we may falter, but our compass will always point us back home.

This insight helps me to be sure that I'm understanding the lessons being presented to me. And this is exactly what most people are telling me they are going through in life.

Pay Up or Payback

Christians don't teach about karma because they believe we only live once, after which we go to either heaven or hell forever—perhaps with an indeterminate stay in purgatory along the way. But karma is real. In some ways, it is like the report card we receive as we move through the world learning life's lessons.

Remember the Golden Rule? Treat others as you would like to be treated—or, said another way, you reap what you sow. But Jesus didn't teach us about the Golden Rule because he couldn't think of anything else to say. He meant it. We are responsible for our actions toward other people and animals. If we don't make amends to those we have hurt, we will experience the consequences. If you don't want to believe in reincarnation, no worries. You don't have to believe you live more than one lifetime to recognize the power and importance of karma. Everything we do has to balance out at some point. If you have hurt others in any way and never made amends while living, you will have to address those actions on the other side or in another lifetime.

Many years ago, I watched a short film by the Edgar Cayce foundation showing a man stealing an ox. Several lifetimes later, someone stole that man's bicycle. This made me look carefully at what I may have done in past lives that I have not taken care of. Rarely do any of us remember our past lives, unless we do so under hypnosis. But it's not necessary to remember, since all our past lives are a part of the Akashic record. If there's something we need to rebalance from our past actions with others, it will show up there. Likewise, if someone has harmed us or taken something from us in a previous life, that will appear as well.

If you have a difficult relationship in your life, and you just cannot figure out what to do with it, it may be worth doing some past-life regression to find out if there are issues that have been carried over from a previous life. Likewise, if you have what seems like an irrational fear, it may be related to how you died in a previous life. Or if you become uncomfortable hearing about certain times in history—for instance, if you are drawn to participate in things like Civil War re-enactments—you may have been alive during those times. Past-life regressions can be very helpful in solving some of your life's mysteries. You can also ask the universe (the Creator) to help you heal and work out issues from former lifetimes. It can even be fun to see what experiences begin to show up that can help you in your healing process.

Our lives are rich with experiences, and some of these involve karmic resolutions. Only when all our karmic lessons have been learned can the soul's purpose for this lifetime be complete. At that point, the physical body dies and the soul moves to the other side—it "graduates," some might say. The death of the physical body may be sad for the loved ones we leave behind, but to the soul it is a new beginning. We get to go back to our heavenly home to rest and to see friends and family who have crossed over. We also get a break from the hectic pace and dense energy of earthly experiences. Yes, we may miss our material lives and our still-living loved ones. We may remember our homes and our pets fondly. Younger souls may even be full of anger about what happened in their lives and about how they died, and that can keep them earthbound. Which, of course, takes us full circle, back to chapter 1.

We all learn through experience. We start out with no consciousness; we create lots of karma; and we move through our subsequent lifetimes learning from our experiences and growing in awareness. We come back again and again, until our souls reach full consciousness. There is a plan for each of our lives.

You can choose to live by the dictates of your mind, or the impulses of your ego, or the controlling power of your will. Or you can choose to live by the messages you receive from that still small voice within— that spark of God's energy that guides you each and every day if you let it. When you do this, you discover the true magic of life.

Message from the Other Side

When I wrote the last sentence of the last chapter, I was relieved that I was done with the many late nights I had spent writing this book. I sent the finished file to my publisher, who then asked me to write a conclusion. Hmmmm, a conclusion. I thought I had said everything I could about living a happily ever after-life. I sat with the request for a few days. Then I realized that, throughout the book, I had given you bits and pieces of my philosophy, but had never pulled the whole picture together for you.

Well, the more I thought about it, the more convinced I became that the best way to end this book was to let my guides do it for me. Here's what my guides had to say when asked at one of my Tuesday classes why we have egos. Their answer explains most of what I have been trying to get across in this book.

Egos protect us. In the first seven years of life, we learn that we need protection. And our egos develop to provide it. Our egos want to be popular, well-liked, well-respected, powerful.

And we observe the adults in our lives to learn what we need. Those whose parents are not strong role models or strong teachers develop an ego out of anger, or frustration, or loneliness—feeling that they have to be warriors, that they have to be out front. So they try to convince others that they are better than everybody else. They try to portray power. Yet, on the inside, they're like jellyfish. They feel no power. They feel no strength. They feel hopeless. They feel betrayed by God for sending them here and, the more betrayed they feel, the bigger and more powerful their egos grow.

In order to live, in order to exist here on this planet, you need an identity, an outside persona that the world sees. The world thinks that that's who you are, and your ego fights hard to protect that image. But that image does not necessarily project the true feelings of the soul. Sometimes the soul just sits back and lets the ego have its way. And sometimes the soul wants to separate itself completely from the ego because it does not express what it feels.

The ego says to the world what it feels the world wants to hear. But in order to grow, the soul must learn to resist the demands of the ego. To the soul, the ego is a form of protection. But to grow, the soul must become more accepting of being vulnerable, of being itself. And that is what a lot of people here on Earth refuse to do—to strip away the ego and present their true selves to the world.

Now, when people come to Earth, they all develop egos. That's just the way it is on this planet. Everyone runs around with their egos out in front. But those who choose to walk a truly spiritual path have to start shaving away the layers of ego that the world has created around them. And by that, we mean that the world has expectations of everyone. It expects certain things from men. It expects certain things from women, and from children, and from elders. There are always expectations. That's the ego at work.

But most people are always trying to find ways to fit in on Earth. They want to be wealthy, or well-liked, or attractive. And that's when the ego starts making judgments about those who aren't fulfilling those expectations. And, because most of the people on this planet just want to get along, they surrender to the ego and ignore their souls.

Life on Earth is tough on the soul. But this is where souls come to grow and to learn. When humans first started coming to Earth, they were just weak little amoebas. And now they've grown from that into the souls that they are today. You've grown, you've gotten stronger, and your consciousness has shifted. And this is good.

You see life more clearly, more easily. You've gotten to the place where you can now choose for yourself what's important and what isn't. You have been here for eons, eons. And now, in this lifetime, you are stripping away the ego so that you can show the world your true self, but you had to go through a lot to accomplish that.

The studying that you've done and the lessons you've learned have been extremely important. Few people want to take this journey. Few are learning to trust. But you are conscious of how you are changing. You are experiencing how easy life can be once you let go of your fear. You are learning that all of your fears have to do only with the ego. Once you become aware of this—once you remove that layer of fear and control—you can live at peace in this graceful place for the rest of your life. This is your opportunity to live in true accordance with your inner voice.

Ego.

Soul.

Every day, you have a choice. Are you going to listen to the strident voice of your ego? Or are you going to listen to the quiet voice of your soul? Are you going to let the world see you as a vulnerable being who is connected to God and lives a conscious life? Or are you going to project the lie that you are invulnerable and that you are in control of your life?

Which will it be?

These are the choices you must make every day on this path. Every day. Like a turtle who loses its shell, you can either focus on how vulnerable you feel, or you can stay focused on your intuitive certainty that you don't need your egoic shell anymore.

We hope you understand what we have just told you.

And so my guides have taught me. And I have tried to pass these lessons along to you. We go on quite a journey to develop ourselves to our highest potential. There's nothing like it in the movies. We are the real deal, and so is this life. Don't let yourself become a ghost hanging out on Earth or on the astral plane. It's such a waste of time and it keeps you back from so much happiness. When you pass out of your body, go straight to that big beautiful light in the sky. It looks like the biggest full moon you'll ever see.

See you on the other side, my friend.

ECHO

ON THE OTHER SIDE

BY MELISSA ANDERSON

This beautiful poem by my friend Melissa Anderson tells of a conversation that a reporter named Jack has with an angel named Bella to get the inside scoop on what's happening on the other side.

Jack: Hey, Bella.

Bella: Hi, Jack! I'm so happy to see you again!

Jack: So, what are you up to today?

Bella: I have a message to deliver to Lucinda on the other side. Want to come with me? I can show you around.

Jack: Sure! Who's Lucinda?

Bella: She's a dear soul. She worked so hard in life that she scarcely had a moment to herself. Now she just rocks in her chair on the porch and waves to the other souls passing by.

Jack: *Sounds like . . . Whoa! Oh, wow! Where are we?*

Bella: *On the other side.*

Jack: *It's gorgeous! The colors! Looks like a big party.*

Bella: *Those are the recent arrivals, reconnecting with their families and friends.*

Jack: *And is that a baseball game over there?*

Bella: *Yup. Bottom of the 42,509,617th inning, bases loaded, two strikes.*

Jack: *So baseball games are interminable over here too.*

Bella: *Those souls never get tired of it. It's their idea of heaven. Let's go over to that mountain stream.*

Jack: *I think I see someone fishing.*

Bella: *There are a lot of souls who are happiest when they have a mountain and a trout stream all to themselves.*

Jack: *So each one of them gets a whole mountain? How does that work?*

Bella: *Well, the mountains don't take up all that much room in infinite space.*

Jack: *What is that mass of lights over there, swooping and dipping in the sky? And do I hear a hum?*

Bella: *Probably. Those are souls who are really into merging with oneness.*

Jack: *They look like a million birds flying in close formation. What are those buildings, the ones without any doors or windows?*

Bella: *Each building is occupied by souls who were very attached to a particular religion or ideology. They assumed they would be the only ones here, so we protect them until they are ready to see more.*

Jack: *What's up with these people who are hauling heavy baggage?*

Bella: *Well, they were told that they had to bring all their stuff—everything they ever did or said or thought—to be sorted and weighed. See, they are emptying their bags onto a scale.*

Jack: *Now they are being handed slips of paper, but they seem confused.*

Bella: *They were hoping for a receipt that would show that the good outweighed the bad, but* instead they get a card that says, "Congratulations on all that you learned in life!"

Jack: Uh, geez, what's that dark place over there?

Bella: (Shuddering) The souls in there are absolutely convinced that they need to be punished. They didn't necessarily do terrible things, but, whatever they did, they are filled with guilt.

Jack: What happens to them?

Bella: We fly through there all the time, hoping their beliefs have changed enough that they can grasp our outstretched hands and break out of there. They all do, eventually.

Jack: Now this is odd. Why are these souls staring at a blank wall?

Bella: They thought that when their lives ended, there would be nothing more—just nothingness. So here they are, seeing nothing.

Jack: How boring.

Bella: Exactly! Boredom is such a blessing here, as on Earth. They finally get tired of nothing and start looking around for something more interesting.

You should see the looks on their faces when that happens.

Jack: *So, what's the deal, Bella? It seems that everyone's heaven is what they want it to be.*

Bella: *Not exactly, Jack. Everyone's heaven is what they believe it will be.*

Jack: *Ah, okay, I get it. Well, I should get back to the office. By the way, what's the message you're delivering to Lucinda?*

Bella: *That her grandson finally believes he's worthy of love.*

Jack: *Sweet!*

Bella: *I know!*

Jack: *Well, gotta go. Always a pleasure, Bella.*

Bella: *Likewise, Jack.*

APPENDIX A: SUMMARY OF LIFE LESSONS

You've just taken in a lot of information, so I thought it might be helpful to summarize the lessons we've explored in this book—not necessarily in their order of importance.

- We all die. None of us gets out of here alive.
- The beliefs we get from our families, society, and religion all play a big role in our lives.
- We go along with everyone else's beliefs because we don't want to rock the boat.
- Your life was well planned, and there are many reasons we are here in this lifetime.
- Our families or lack of family helps us fulfill our destiny.
- A good numerologist or astrologer can help you understand your path. (Find someone who is advanced in their training and knowledge.)

- We are striving to look at life through the eyes of the victor and not the victim
- It helps to look at each experience as a teacher. What is this teaching me?
- The expression "what we resist persists" is true. Is there an addiction that you're dealing with? Can you work on recovering from it?
- It is important to make amends for the hurt you have caused others and to forgive those who have hurt you. When you're on the other side, you will understand what that relationship was about.
- Death is the ending of your current adventure here on Earth, but that adventure definitely continues on the other side.
- If you are physically, mentally, or emotionally challenged in this life, it is not God's fault. It was part of your life's plan.
- Remember that everyone who is more than an acquaintance in this life is someone significant from a previous life. You may have a karmic debt to resolve.

- Remember to live according to the Golden Rule with everyone in your life. Treat everyone as you would like to be treated.

- Ending a relationship too soon without completing what you need to complete may bring the two of you back together again. Quick marriages are often the result of unfinished business in a past life.

- Focus on learning compassion for others rather than making judgments. Whatever we judge, we will have to experience ourselves at some future time.

- No one can escape the law of karma.

- Have a personal relationship with God. Talk to God just as you would talk to your best friend.

- Listen to the still small voice within and follow its guidance. Living by intuition, which is the silent voice of God, takes away a lot of the fear we carry around. When you talk to God, you discover that you are not alone in your life.

- Think of the Earth as a school and every experience here as a classroom in which to learn.

- Don't stop growing just because you are older or incapacitated. Take advantage of being alive and keep learning new things.
- Just as a brand new baby looks for the light as it comes out of the womb, look for the light as you are returning home from the school of life.
- Karma applies to animals as well. Treat them with love.
- Get your affairs in order so that, when you do go over to the other side, you won't fret about all the things you forgot to do.
- Don't be afraid of death.

APPENDIX B:
PROFESSIONAL REFERRALS

Click on the link below to find all the vendors that work at my teaching center: psychics, healers, astrologers, numerologists, Akashic records, inner-child work, jewelry, rocks, clearing products, and more.

www.virtualspiritualitycenter.com

Books and meditation CDs are available at

echobodine.com

ABOUT THE AUTHOR

In 1981, Echo began teaching classes on psychic development and spiritual healing. She has appeared on numerous national television shows, including *The Sally Jesse Raphael Show, Sightings, Beyond, The Other Side, Unexplained Mysteries, The Today Show,* and *Encounters. Paranormal Borderline* did a feature story on her family, calling them the "world's most psychic family." She has also been a guest on numerous radio shows throughout the country, including *Coast to Coast.*

Echo has hosted her own cable TV show, called *New Age Perspectives,* as well as her own radio show in Minneapolis, called *Intuitive Living.* Paramount Pictures solicited her services for the promotion of the movie *Ghost.*

From 2003 to the present, Echo has been the director of The Center for Intuitive Living, where she teaches numerous classes on spiritual development,

living by intuition, ghostbusting, psychic development, and laying-on-hands healing. In 2010, she
began doing online psychic development and intuition classes. She is a field representative for the
Edgar Cayce A.R.E., and has a bi-monthly podcast
with Bobby Sullivan called *Intuitive Living*.

I found an old picture of you.
(Photo by ESAHubble & NASA)

Hampton Roads Publishing Company

. . . for the evolving human spirit

Hampton Roads Publishing Company
publishes books on a variety of subjects,
including spirituality, health, and
other related topics.

For a copy of our latest trade catalog, call
(978) 465-0504 or visit our distributor's website at
www.redwheelweiser.com. You can also sign up for
our newsletter and special offers by going to
www.redwheelweiser.com/newsletter/.